RESTART

Escaping Anxiety and Fear

Dr. Steve Smith

ISBN: 978-1-941000-13-7

http://www.ChurchEquippers.com

This is for my next generation—

Zack, Ian, Atari, Piers, John...and all that come after them.

Special thanks to Evie Digirolamo, who made me learn and grow in my ability to write.

Glory to God alone.

CONTENTS

BEFORE YOU START...

YOU ONLY HAVE ONE LIFE

How do you want to live it?

"LIFE IS WHAT happens to you while you are busy making other plans." sang John Lennon. Your life is happening right now. The question for you is, do you want to choose how it will be shaped or are you just going to let it turn out however it does?

Perhaps you have not thought much about your future self. You are living in the world of tests, Instagram, video games, hanging out with friends, preparing for college or working a part-time job. SATs are looming in the coming year or so. Maybe you are already taking college classes and juggling your study and party time with a job. Or perhaps you have chucked the whole school scene to learn a trade, possibly even working in the family business.

Maybe you have darker pursuits, doing things that are edgy, secret and harmful. You find yourself wishing that you could restart your life, have better friends—have more hope in your life. Hope that you will escape the nagging worry that grays the color out of your life. Hope that you will not be forever crushed by the weight of the bad things that have already happened to you. Hope that you will live, if not happily ever after, a better life than the one you are living now.

I am not talking about your future career or marriage or education choices. I am speaking about something much deeper than that. I am speaking about the essential you—who you are, what you choose that shapes your thinking and what you will do. More to the point, what you choose to do about the emotions inside you that could lead you well or seek to destroy you and your best life at every turn—raging emotions like anxiety and fear.

Unaddressed, they will wield far greater power than they have the right to. People allow these negative emotions to drive their life into the ditch all the time.

Ethan chose to allow his damaged emotions to take charge. His father left his mother when he was in grade school. The resulting feelings of abandonment led to rebellion and driving away friends because he resented their normal family life. He took up with miserable guys like him, seeking to make others miserable as a way of evening the score. His sudden marriage and the child that followed before he was out of high school put pressure on him to make a living. He worked one minimum wage job after another, barely keeping food on the table and a roof over his head.

His anxiety and fears continued to drive him further down a self-destructive road. He slept with other women and drove a wedge between himself and all the adults who wanted to help him—or at least his wife and child.

Then one day, God woke him up. He saw he was full of addictive behaviors that were the results of his choices. He wanted a better life before he grew any older, but was not sure how to undo what he had done to himself. He chose to seek out a person he had pushed away in the past and began to learn how to have his damaged emotions healed by God's Spirit. He is on a path to be set free from the destructive behaviors he had been living out.

What I learned from knowing Ethan's story is two things. First, being blind to the driving force of unhealthy emotions will bring you a lot of present—as well as future—misery. Second, it is never too late to restart. You do not have to live out the worst version of yourself.

Your choice.

Hope is what this book is about. Hope that you can come to know and see healed what's eating you up inside. Hope for a better, brighter future than the one you may see developing now.

I will introduce you to a journey that I have been on already for many years. It will become your life-long journey as well. It is about you and God. I am not going to talk about believing in Jesus so you can go to heaven. I am going to talk about believing Jesus so you can live right now here on Earth. Live in freedom—in wholeness through the stresses of life—empowered every day by God's Spirit.

Even if you regularly attend church, you may not know that this is what the good news about Jesus is all about. But it is. And I want you to know this before you have to look back with regret on your life. I want you to be able to move forward in your life armed with the truth Jesus taught that will set you free.

Steve Smith

1. THE JOURNEY

YOU HAVE UNFINISHED BUSINESS

MY SISTER WAS screaming. I had just hit her—hard. My mom, hearing the commotion in the kitchen, rushed in to break it up. I blamed my sister. She blamed me. But I had a history of this kind of thing. With a voice filled with frustration, mom snapped at me, "Listen to me Steve. You better get that temper of yours under control or you are heading for a lot of trouble."

My mother was right on target. But I didn't know it then. The trouble was still simmering. The full explosion didn't happen until I was much older.

But my mom's words stung. And I was confused. What temper? And what about my sister's part of it? Why do I always get all the blame?

Thinking back now, I don't even know why I hit my sister. I was just mad.

I did not want to keep getting into trouble, because trouble with Mom meant bigger trouble with Dad when he got home from work. And the thought of being in trouble with my dad scared me into taking Mom seriously. So I did exactly what she suggested—I got that temper of mine under control. I'd hide out in my room when I felt explosive. I became a loner so I could avoid getting into fights with family members. I leashed it up like a wolfhound, not knowing that you cannot leash it up forever. Anger, like every other addictive power in life, will eventually chew through the leash and bite you in the butt.

I was thirteen when people began to label me as having a bad temper. To be honest, I knew deep down that I was angry. But I had no idea *why* I was angry. It wasn't my sister or my brothers or the kids in the neighborhood or my teachers at school. I thought that in order to control my temper, I had to somehow stop being angry without having to deal with where the anger was coming from. That meant I could only stuff the anger down, not end it. This turned out to be a recipe for disaster later in my life.

After a long painful journey to find the source of my deep anger, I look back on that day and wish I had known what I know now. We do and say wrong things because we live with fears and anxieties inside…everyone…even people who belong to Jesus.

The anxieties and fears you have inside you are a product of hurts, wounds, and traumas that happened to you since you were born and even while you were in your mother's womb. But that's not all. Humans are wired to avoid pain. So when you felt the pain of these hurts, you tried to comfort them by making damaging choices. Choices that you did not know you made. But the combination of these hurts and your choices are wreaking havoc in your life.

What you have is what I call unfinished business—pain-filled life experiences that you have not yet dealt with—but need to. And you will need help learning how to do that, because few people know what to do about their unfinished business. Left unaddressed, it tears apart our lives, our families, our friendships and our walk with God.

To address your unfinished business, you have to become aware of what the real problem is. When you're sick and go to a doctor, she wants to know what your symptoms are so she can diagnose the true illness. For example, your stuffed up nose is not really your problem. The virus attacking your upper respiratory tract is the problem. You can blow your nose, use nasal spray, or dry out the mucus all you want, but your stuffiness won't go away until the virus is killed. The stuffy nose is just the symptom, not the problem.

The reason you are not getting over your anxieties and fears is because you are spending your time trying to fix the symptoms instead of the illness. You might think that your anger or depression or your unhappiness at home or lack of friends is your problem. Not at all. They are just the symptoms. And trying to fix just the symptoms leads to frustration.

What are your symptoms? Maybe you are angry like I was. You get into fights at school and at home, and have a reputation of being tough or a rebel. Or you hold on to grudges and have a deep bitterness against someone, perhaps a former friend. Possibly you've joined a gang looking for trouble, which will damage your life even more than it is damaged now.

Or perhaps you are not angry, but feel lonely and cannot seem to find a true friend. Or you had a good friend, but your behavior drove him or her away. Or you can't find someone to go out with you who likes you for yourself. You pretend you don't care, but you do care a lot.

Or maybe you are doing destructive stuff, like bullying others and destroying property that belongs to others. Or stealing. Perhaps you are caught up in pornography or have started having sex, even with people you do not really care about. Or maybe you're cutting yourself.

Or when you talk to yourself, you call yourself "stupid" or "worthless" or "ugly" or "useless." You have come to the conclusion that no one is ever going to like you because of the way you are. You hate yourself. And you are convinced you cannot change. Perhaps you are even thinking you should just kill yourself.

On the other hand, you may be on the top of the heap and looking down on others. Your competitive ways are not kind. You privately (or not so privately) gloat over being better than others. You like showing off. You feel very little sympathy for people who don't have what you have.

Did you see yourself in this list of symptoms? If not, there are more. Whatever your personal symptoms are, however, they are not your problem. They are the visible sign of the anxiety and fear—the unfinished business—in your life.

So why haven't you gotten help as soon as you became aware of your anxieties and fears? The first reason is, like me, you probably never connected what you feel to why you act, think and say the things you do. Your best guess now might be that it has something to do with the way you were raised, something to do with your dad and mom—or your siblings—or someone else. But you're not sure, and there is no one you trust enough to help you how to find out.

The second reason you haven't gotten help is the pain you feel inside. Some of you have tried to discover why you're not handling life very well. But you found that when that wound that was inside you was exposed, it hurt really bad—unbearably bad. And it makes you feel more anxious every time you think about it. So much so, that you would rather go to the dentist and get a tooth drilled without Novocain than face that kind of pain and anxiety. So you have left it alone.

Then there is the fear—that you will have to repeatedly experience the intense pain that is at the root of your anxiety. The lie Satan adds is, "Alone." After all, who would you talk to that you could trust? Perhaps you tried before and got stabbed in the back. Or maybe told it was all in your head. Or you got shut down by someone in authority who really didn't bother to listen to you. But since you are reading this, let me suggest that you have not quite closed the door on the hope that there is help somewhere for you.

I was almost forty years old before I learned what I am going to share with you. The wolfhound by now had gnawed through the leash and I had become an increasingly out of control angry man. Every day I woke up ready to be mad about something and at someone—particularly at the ones I was living with, my wife and children.

I had uprooted my family from their secure life in Wisconsin to help start something new in Florida. My kids were upset because they had to leave their friends. We couldn't move into the home we were building when we got here, forcing us to scramble for a place to stay for several months. Living in chaos. I had hardly caught my breath before my business partner pulled the trigger to start the new venture, literally the day after I arrived. I felt overstretched trying to take care to make sure my resentful family was okay while running around sixteen or more hours a day to get things lined up for the grand opening. I was exhausted.

Besides this, I was working with a very creative person who was traveling out of the area regularly, popping up sometimes only a couple of days a week with decisions that had to be carried out right now! I am wired to need time to think and plan before I do things, so I felt pressured to jump when he said jump. I felt that I was not really being treated like an equal partner. And I felt madder and madder as time went by.

And remember, I was already an angry man. I was yelling at my kids more and forcing them to do extra chores that only made them more resentful. And I started complaining out loud about my partner to everyone inside our organization, letting them know how he was messing up and being a jerk—instead of going to him and working things out.

The final straw was the day he and I sat in a restaurant while he talked to me about what I needed to learn to be a better partner. Me a better partner? What about him?!!!

I lost it. All the anger that had been building up in me blew up like the volcano I had become. The people in that part of the restaurant cleared out. My anger kept me raging for weeks.

Finally out of desperation I went to see a counselor who listened to me pour out my hurt and frustration. After listening to me for four hours, he told me to do something that both surprised me and started me on a journey that changed my life.

DEEP CHANGE

If you are going to get free of your unfinished business, start by accepting that you cannot change yourself. I cannot do it. You cannot do it. None of us can make ourselves become what God created us to be. I know that this frustrates a lot of people. People want to believe they can fix themselves. So they try different strategies that others have used before them—none of which really work.

One is playing Pretend. This is acting as if nothing is wrong, nothing bad has happened in your life. So you go around pretending that "I'm happy!" "I've got this!" What this person is working hard to do is create a fairytale world that has more of a Disney quality to it than Grimm.

Lots of people around you are playing pretend. They are crying behind their eyes, aching in their hearts and anxious about life all the time, while putting up a front that they have it all together. They pretend they are okay and even try to make people believe they are problem free.

Pretending your life is okay will not take away what is underneath. You can put your reality in a box and stuff it into the back of your inner closet, but you cannot escape its influence on you. Pain will out. Bad choices you made in the past will show up at your parties, enter college with you and chaperone every date you go on. Because, what is inside you has been hardwired to your soul and can only be removed by the One who made you, whether or not you deny that pain exists.

You might try the strategy of making a Lateral Move. Lateral moves are about moving sideways from your anxieties and fears, seeking to find a happy place through some kind of change. Perhaps you change friends, or you change your relationship with your group from normal to being an outsider to being an insider and back again. Or you change your looks, or change where you live as soon as you can, thinking that putting distance between you and your family is the ticket. Maybe you change from being a good person into a rule-breaking rebel. Or change the person you are dating, thinking this new person will make the difference.

Lateral moves never really work because wherever you go, you find that you and all your anxieties have come with you. Seeking a happy place is fruitless because it involves moving sideways instead of going forward towards health, no matter what that journey costs.

Maybe you have already indulged in playing the Blame Game. This strategy is as old as the Bible. It tells you that someone messed you up, hurt you, deprived you in some way—and, buddy, that person owes you. You want them to suffer for what they did. Or to confess that they are the reason for your unhappiness in life. If they would just own up to their guilt, you think you would be okay, be whole again.

We have all been damaged by others. But the blame game (which I will talk more about in the next chapter) will never set you free. So hear this now. While you did not deserve to be damaged by other people, focusing your life on waiting for them to confess their wrongs and beg your forgiveness will keep you stuck for life.

A final strategy you might be using to try to escape your unfinished business is to become religious. You might go to church, obey the pastor and try to follow what the Bible says, hoping you will be changed. Because this sounds like something God would want you to do, you may be confused and disappointed when nothing changes. You still feel anxious, still have unanswered questions and are now beginning to wonder if there really is a God.

Many of your friends are faking it at church. They are hurting too, but they want to believe that going to church will make their lives different. Becoming religious is *almost* right, which is why it is so wrong.

Why doesn't it work? It doesn't work because religion can be an expression of our devotion to God, but it is not the same as knowing God Himself and letting Him transform you. This kind of relationship involves honesty and humility. And as you read on I will tell you how to have the kind of relationship with Him that will set you free.

All these strategies fail because they cover up the unhappiness and hurt, but they never tackle it. God is offering you much more than just muddling through life in misery and confusion. He is offering deep change. Deep change brought about by God so that your inner desires—desires that direct how you make life choices—are changed. Deep change that transforms your character. This is much more than an attitude adjustment that would make you a more likeable person. Deep change allows you to become the person you were created to be. It is not about what you should do, but about what you will become. Deep change is not, "I should be less anxious, so I will work at being less anxious." Instead, it is "I will be changed into the peace-filled person I was made to be and am not yet."

This is a book about a restart, about changing your life—about being transformed. How God will free you from your fears and anxieties. It's about what He will do to heal and deliver you from what is damaging you. I will tell you about the path you will need to take to get there, one which I learned so late in life.

WHAT BEING TRANSFORMED MEANS

Being transformed is different than reforming your behavior. Reforming your behavior is about changing how you act, but it never gets down into how you think and feel. You reform yourself because it keeps you out of trouble with your family or teachers, helps you fit into your group, or opens doors of privilege you didn't have when you were acting badly.

I was a 'know it all' growing up. I corrected teachers who got facts wrong right in front of the class. I argued with friends because I knew better than they did. I was smarter than they were and I let them know it. This was very satisfying to me.

That is…until the day when one of my friends told me the truth about how my know-it-all practices ticked people off. I was losing friends because of it. So I reformed myself by learning to bite my tongue and I stopped correcting others. But that didn't stop me from feeling smug inside every time they made a mistake!

Maybe you have done something like this too. But reforming yourself is not what I am going to teach you. God is not demanding that you reform by stop being anxious or fearful. He is going to do that for you! He is going to use His power to change you on the inside. And when you are changed on the inside, you no longer want to act stupid or ugly or mean or messy.

The difference between reforming and being transformed is this:

Reforming yourself: Acting like Jesus by hearing God's truth and trying to obey in your own power.

Being transformed: Acting like Jesus by hearing God's truth and *trusting in the Spirit's power* to do this *for* you.

That is what transformation is all about. It comes from a relationship with God that involves the Spirit, who lives in you, empowering you to live a better kind of life.

My counselor listened to me go on and on about my anger, then said, "Steve, there is no doubt things have been done to you that were wrong. But you are way too angry for this to be about your partner. I believe that God is using your partner as a hammer and chisel to open up your soul for healing." That stunned me. Then he challenged, "Get alone with God for as long as it takes and ask Him this question, "Why am I angry?"

This was not the advice I had expected. I thought I was supposed to ask God to *take my anger away*. It never crossed my mind to ask Him to show me where it came from. But my anger had become scary, so that week I found a place to be alone with God.

I sat with a notepad and pen in hand while I asked God to show me why. During that time, God showed me the pain of my past that I was carrying inside me. All my life I felt no one valued me. I felt no one thought I was worth investing time in. No one noticed my potential. I felt worthless. As a result, I felt that other people did not really respect or care about me.

I finally understood how I had never let God heal that part of my life. As a result, I had chosen anger to cover the hurt. But the hurt continued to hurt and the need for more and more anger to bring comfort increased until I was addicted to anger.

I asked God that day to heal me, to transform the 'angry me' in a way no one else, not even I, could do. Healing started that day. Before long I stopped being an angry person. The anger did not go away because I worked hard at it. It went away all by itself as God healed me within of what was really hurting and causing me to be anxious about life.

So what are the root causes of your anxiety? That is what this book is going to help you to discover. You probably got your unfinished business in a different way from how I and other people got theirs. I have a friend who was bullied growing up in Cuba because his dad would not join the Communist party. He was a target for being beaten up and he carried that anxiety for years. A Haitian friend grew up in a country that hated his nationality and it skewed his acceptance of himself.

Your story will be different. Maybe you have experienced sexual abuse or neglect or unjust punishment or poverty or shaming. Yet whatever your story of how you became anxious, the restart process, the way to becoming whole again is the same.

SURRENDERING TO THE PROCESS

I am going to explain to you a lot about what is going on inside you. But please understand, you do not have to wait until you are forty, or thirty or even twenty, to deal with what is unfinished in you. This is exactly why I am writing this book, so you do not have to wait until you are destroying your life like I was.

I am going to teach you three things that matter for your life. The first thing will be how your life got messed up. I will start by showing you in the Bible how this whole story began. Then I will help you to explore ways in which you have been wounded, hurt and traumatized—I will not be teaching you to point fingers here as much as learning to identify where your anxieties and fears came from. Then I will teach you about internal choices you have made that have a great deal to do with why you are stuck.

Secondly, I will bring you to the one question that matters if you are going to get free of your unfinished business. It is a simple question Jesus once asked, but everyone who wants to be transformed has to answer it at some point.

Finally, I will show you how to pursue intimacy with God. What you will read may be very different from what you have heard from other people. You will find it challenging. Maybe it will sound a little weird, but it won't *feel* weird once you start. Knowing and trusting God is at the heart of becoming the person you want to be and living the life you hope to live.

It's about a living relationship with God. One that grows and transforms as you grow and are transformed. No one changes deeply without knowing God better. Without knowing God better, no one sees him- or herself clearly enough to understand what needs to change. And a lack of understanding will keep you from surrendering to the deep change you need.

Here's the deal. If you have gained any hope through what you have read so far, why not risk going on? It takes courage to do this. I say courage because you must be willing to submit to God's ruthless searching in the hidden places of your soul. You will need to say, "Search me, O God, and know my heart; test me and know my anxious thoughts. Point out anything in me that offends you, and lead me along the path of everlasting life" (Psalm 139:23-24 NLT). I will come back to this later.

Are you ready? Will you accept the challenges necessary to get there? If so, let me guide you on this journey to freedom.

2. THE STARTING POINT

YOUR JOURNEY STARTS WITH THE TRUTH

I LEARNED ALL the stories in the Bible when I was a kid. Its very first story explains why we are anxious and fearful. This story also tells us why everybody is so damaged. And more importantly, the story reveals what God intended to do to restore us back to wholeness.

To become whole, you have to grasp some basic truths. These truths have always been true. They were true for your parents. They were true for your grandparents—and your great-grandparents. They were just as true for the people who lived in the Stone Age as they are for us who live in the age of the Internet. Every life has been affected by this one story, which has had a profound and lasting effect on the human race.

This story is referred to as the Fall. It is a pretty simple one. It's about Adam and Eve being created and placed in a perfect place called Eden, in a perfect relationship with each other, with nature and with

God. All they had to do was to not eat from one tree. A sneaky talking snake appeared who encouraged Eve to eat forbidden fruit, saying it would make her like God. Attracted to the fruit because of the power promised, she munched some down. Then she gave some to the man and he wolfed it down too. After they both ate the fruit, they immediately found the need for clothes. Judgment from God followed, resulting in the first human pair getting kicked out of the garden with curses all around for the man, woman, and the snake. Problems galore followed.

As simple as the story is, it shouts out the most basic truths about what is wrong with us. When God created Adam, then Eve, he gave them freedom to do and say all that entered their minds. The relationship between God and the human pair was open and clear. They and God had an intimate friendship. Nothing was hidden between them. In fact, breaking this relationship is the most crucial part of this story.

So what was the big deal of the story? God told them they were not allowed to eat fruit off the Tree of the Knowledge of Good and Evil. If they did, they would really die. The serpent, who is Satan, came to Eve and said in effect, "God lied to you, you won't really die." This is the first time in the Bible that humans get confused by Satan's lies.

Do you remember when you first questioned whether your parents could be trusted in everything they said? Or a time when they said they did not trust you—and you were hurt? This is exactly the way Eve was feeling as Satan offered alternative facts about the tree. God cannot be trusted. God is trying to keep you down. God knows if you eat the fruit from this tree, your eyes will be opened. Then you will be able to make your own decisions about what is right and wrong.

Satan lied. Eve bit. Then Adam bit also when she handed him some of the tree's fruit.

And their eyes were opened. But not in the way they hoped. They expected to have this amazing becoming-like-a-god experience, when they would know deep truth for themselves. Instead, they saw *themselves*—that they were naked. They felt ashamed.

While it is tempting to focus on their lack of clothes, this is not what this part of the story is about. What they realized in that moment is that they needed to hide. Up to this point, they had been totally transparent with each other. They shared everything—without fear. But from here on out, they felt the need to hide their bodies. Hide their thoughts. Hide their secrets. Hide their mistakes. Their decision to mistrust God caused them to hide in the bushes when they heard Him coming.

Their soul—and ours too—was permanently damaged. They were broken at the deepest level. And…they had no way to undo their choice. When their eyes were opened, they realized they were messed up. They now suffered unexpected fear in their most important relationship. They probably wanted a do-over. And yet, the lie was like a song that gets stuck in your head. "God can't be trusted. God can't be trusted."

You and I have no idea what it is like to live totally whole and safe with God like Eve and Adam did before the Fall. They discovered in the twinkling of an eye that they had secrets to keep from God and from each other. Putting on fig leaf clothes was more than a fashion statement. It shouted 'I'm hiding stuff' loud and clear.

I don't know about you, but of all the friends I have, I never, not even in my closest relationships, have experienced a time when one of us wasn't hiding something from the other. You can't be open with others because that will mean rejection. Or you keep your secrets because they might give someone else—parents, teachers, false friends—power over you. You may have learned this the hard way. Some of you know this instinctively.

Yet this is exactly what causes painful anxiety inside you. Your most basic desire is to be loved unconditionally by others, no matter what. Right now you are looking for this kind of love, whether or not you realize it. Or you are despairing of finding it, because you have probably already discovered that human love is conditional. You usually have to earn it, and if you aren't careful you can lose it. So people will love you only if you hide the full truth about yourself. And you think God does not—could not—love you either. Not the full you. This is one of the terrible outcomes of this story.

DOING WHAT WE PLEASE

Another outcome with huge consequences is that Adam and Eve got what they wanted. They got the knowledge of good and evil. But it didn't work out as they thought it would. Not for them. And it hasn't for us.

Yes, we grow up and believe we can make the right choices for our lives. Everyone thinks that they know what is good and what is evil. But here's the mess Adam and Eve got us into—none of us share the same meaning for good and evil. No one in your family shares your exact definitions. Neither do your friends, although you are drawn to people who mostly agree with you. But in the big wide world, the majority disagrees with your good/evil categories. There are whole groups who disagree and they will do everything in their power to make you bend to their views. Think about how people you know differ on politics or immigrants or what it means to be racist or just and unjust laws. These are just the tip of the iceberg about how deeply motivated people are to make you see the view of good and evil in the world their way.

That is the problem. Even while you are practicing your own version of godhood, everyone else is doing the same. This is what is called being free to do or believe whatever you want. Everyone wants their own way. Everyone wants to be the boss over everyone else's life. And you want to live your own truth, to be happy doing what pleases you, which often adds to the tension people feel toward you at home, at school and in the places you hang out.

Mom and Dad make rules that drive us crazy. Brothers and sisters try to order us around. Teachers, security personnel, kids from other neighborhoods, athletes, cops, shopkeepers, people from other cultures seek to control us. Some hurt us, violate us, and rob life of its joy. Sometimes this is unconsciously done by them. Sometimes it is meant to be cruel, mean and dehumanizing. People use you. People hurt you and don't care. They do as they please.

And what is worse, you are doing this to others too. You do what you want and ignore the consequences. You find that you cannot—and do not want to—stop doing what you want no matter who gets hurt. It's triggered in you as naturally as the sun rising in the east. You do what pleases you without hitting the pause button to think about it.

What is more, you find that doing what pleases you is like a drug. After a while you are addicted. Even when you know what you are going to do will harm someone, even yourself, you cannot stop. Dad and Mom cannot make you stop. Laws cannot stop you. Knowing people disapprove cannot stop you. Knowing there is a God cannot stop you.

It's kind of like owning a smartphone. Smartphones aren't evil. But after a while, you might find that you have your head bent and nose pointed into it continually. You stop talking to your friends directly. Meal times are used to check apps. Conversation becomes non-existent. The number of people involved in accidents while texting and walking is going up. All of us have seen the signs that say, "Don't text and drive!" Why do we need these signs? Because a very good device—a smartphone—has become a drug-like activity for so many people. And though we know this, we can't stop ourselves from grabbing a peek while hurtling down the road behind the wheel of a car. People can't stop themselves. This is addiction.

Now here is the bad news. *Anything* in your life can take control of how you feel and act. Anger can lead you to battle everyone around you. Lying can become your native tongue. Stabbing people in the back can become a lifestyle.

Addiction causes friendships to break. People hold secret grudges against you. Trust is lost. Doing what pleases you has a set of teeth that will someday (maybe already has) leave wicked bite marks on your soul.

The problem is you do not understand your decision-maker—which the Bible calls the heart. Jeremiah 17:9 (MSG) says that, "The heart is hopelessly dark and deceitful, a puzzle that no one can figure out." If you desire to become a healthy soul, you have to understand why you're making the decisions you're making. But probably you don't even recognize that many of the doing-what-pleases-me choices you make are damaging to you and others.

You may think your choices are natural, normal. Others choose what you choose. Why shouldn't you do it? What's wrong with your choices, your way of living? This is the deception of your heart that Jeremiah is speaking about.

Possibly you realize you are not really free, even as you argue you are free. You say you are in control, you're living the life you want, and you only live once. Right? But really whatever you have chosen is now controlling you, whether you chose a lifestyle, relationships, fantasies, food, spending money, alcohol, recreation, cruelty, or one of an endless host of other things. Your unfinished business—the ways you chose to cover up pain—has become your identity and your worst enemy at the same time. You are being robbed of the ability to love and be loved by God and others.

How can you tell? Here are some telltale signs.

- You are not sleeping at night.
- Certain activities you've been okay with are now causing problems for you and causing fights with your family.
- You are giving far too much time and unhealthy emotion to certain relationships in your life.
- The new activity you tried has not made you stop hurting inside.

- Past events of your life, which you have duct-taped up and hidden away in your inner closet, are now peeking out and screaming for attention.
- The things you own no longer distract you from the emptiness you feel inside.

The truth you cannot escape is how deeply you have been affected by the Fall—the rejection by Adam and Eve of God's right to reign over them. Doing what you please has affected everything—all your decisions, hopes, dreams, activities, thoughts, and relationships. There is nothing you do or touch that is not messed up by the Fall.

THE BLAME GAME BEGINS

To deal with all your hurt and confusion, you may now be playing the oldest game in the book—the blame game—your problems are somebody else's fault.

We have to go back to the Garden story to find where this started. Adam and Eve eat the forbidden fruit. They change instantly from loving, open partners to uneasy competitors. Then they hear God coming. They hide. When God asks the obvious question, "Why?" Adam points his finger at anyone but himself. In fact, Adam shows an immediate mastery of the blame game. He chooses to put the blame on both God, who gave him Eve as a partner, and Eve herself. God does not stop to debate the point with Adam, but turns to the woman for her view of the situation. She follows Adam's lead. 'The snake did it.'

This game, as you see, does not need to be taught to you. It's built in. So whose fault is it that you have unfinished business? If you are human you already are blaming someone else. Someone in your world has to be—is!—at fault. It's your dad's, mom's, sister's, brother's—someone's—fault that you ended up with these issues. Or like Adam, you blame God. He failed you. He did not protect you. He burdened you with the handicap, problem, hurt, or violation you have lived with all these years. Maybe that's why you don't want anything to do with God anymore, and any of the others that landed you into this mess.

You can go on blaming God or other people for your life. There is nothing to stop you. No lecture, no law or pressure can be applied by anyone to make you change your mind about who's at fault for your unfinished business. But understand that you will not only stay stuck in your situation, it will get worse as time passes. Unfinished business is not about the past alone. It affects your present and will continue to create chaos in your future. The blame game is a smoke screen keeping your eyes blinded to the way out. All it offers is the false comfort that you are not responsible.

Lakisha is someone who is stuck this way. Her life revolved around her own drama. Because of her self-centeredness, she had made an incredibly bad choice to break up with her long-time boyfriend, then bitterly regretted it when he took up with someone else. She has pushed away the closest people in her life because they were the ones she blamed for her messed-up choice. They were the ones she accused of conspiring to hurt her. They did not take her side and give her justice. They were mean to her. They were unfair. And so she ended up alone and sad in a world of her own making.

If you are going to go on a healing journey, you must accept that it is you who made the life choices that make up your unfinished business. You chose how you would deal with the pain. That what you have become is the result of your choices. You have to take responsibility for your choices or you will not start the journey to become whole. I will add more about this later.

THE GOOD NEWS

The Garden story is not just a tragedy. It is also a hope-filled story as well. If God had handed out complete justice, Eve and Adam would have experienced total annihilation. Instead, God reveals His heart. Speaking to the snake first, God says in effect that conflict will become the way of life between the snake (who is Satan) and humankind, but that a descendent of the woman will eventually defeat him even though the snake will try to destroy that person. The rest of the Bible is the unfolding of this promise. This is the beginning of the story of how God would make a way for us to become whole again through the death and life of Jesus, God generously provided this pathway back for all of us through sacrificial love even though we don't deserve it. Knowing this truth is also critical for anyone who wants a healthy soul.

What is it that we learn about God's love in this story? First, that God's love is *action*, not *feelings*. Our love for a number of people in our lives is limited to what we feel. Our emotions tell us whether we are in love or not. We hope that the person we love feels the same about us and feel sorrow or hurt when our love is not returned. This is not so for God. He *chooses* to love. God demonstrates it by actively loving those who really do not care for Him at all. This kind of love is a willful love—a decision to act for the good of those He loves even when they don't love him back. What this part of the story tells us is how deeply God loves those He created. *He* is the one who made a way for people to be reconciled to Him. Instead of expecting people to figure out what they needed to do to repair their relationship with God, He sets out a plan where he does all the heavy lifting for us.

The second feature of God's love found here is that He loves even when we spit in his face. Your love for someone probably wouldn't survive if that person stabbed you in the back for no reason and didn't even feel bad about it. Perhaps you know this through personal experience.

But God does not respond as people do. And not just with Adam and Eve. God knows the worst about you and me. He sees past the pretty face we put over our broken soul and He never stops loving us. Nothing is hidden from Him—not even our darkest secrets covered by our most sincere lies. Nothing stops Him from loving us.

Let me hasten to add that His love will not keep us from the consequences of our choices. Adam and Eve ate the forbidden fruit. They were told what the results would be, but still they ate. The consequences that followed—the judgments, the loss of Eden as home, and the running down of their life's clock—were no surprises, even though they were sorry that they received them.

We are just like them. We make life choices all the time that come with consequences we would rather not receive. Does that stop us? No. And then when the consequences happen we get angry at God. We feel they are too harsh, too unfair. Since we are sorry we think that it's only fair that they be lifted. But seldom do those unhappy consequences just go away.

There is purpose in the pain of consequences. The pain drives us towards God. To be clear, we are not being punished by God. The actions we chose had built-in penalties, like the one Adam and Eve already knew about before they took the first bite. But it is these very penalties that remind us we are the created beings, not the Creator. We cannot fix what we and others have caused to go wrong. We need someone to rescue us from the mess we have made for ourselves, someone powerful who loves us in spite of the fact we do not love Him.

This leads to the third characteristic of God's love in the Garden story. God is not interested in cheap forgiveness. Cheap forgiveness is saying, "You're forgiven." without doing the hard work of repairing the broken relationship caused by our brokenness. God is not the kind of person who is okay with the damage you have done to yourself.

We do matter to God. He knows how stuck and out of control we are. That's why this story includes God's decision about how to rescue and restore humankind after we messed up. Our very lives were at stake. Adam and Eve and all their descendants were now the walking dead, living under the curse of the penalty of death. "I forgive you." would not overturn death. Death as a consequence had to be paid. So God chose to take their consequence on Himself by dying in their place. In doing so He demonstrated not only His love but also His mercy. Though we rebelled, God chooses to forgive us and to free us from the damage done to us by our own choices.

Here is the truth about love. Your deepest desire is to be loved. The love you are looking for in life is God. Not just because God is loving but because God is Love. He himself is the definition of love. All His actions towards you are rooted in love. Does this sound like someone who is disappointed in you?—absolutely not.

Your needs are driving you towards God, not away from God. The dividing issue between you and God is about who is going to be in charge. You can choose to run your own life instead of receiving God's love. The result will be that you will try to find love somewhere else or in someone else. Try as you might, when you look for love apart from God, who is the source of love, you will not be heading towards becoming a healthy person.

God's love for you tops what you may feel about yourself at this moment. Perhaps you have no love for yourself. Inside you is the pain of self-hatred or the feeling that you are a failure or worse. While you may not be able to believe this at the moment, God who created you values you more than you do. He who created you is unfailing in His love for you in spite of all the warts you have developed.

WE HAVE BEEN GIVEN EVERYTHING WE NEED FOR THE JOURNEY

So where is all this leading? I hope you do not believe this is about becoming more religious, or following more rules, or working harder to make yourself better. Those kinds of activities are not going to help you to become a healthy soul.

No!—where this is leading is towards a deeper more intimate relationship with God. You need a deeper understanding of God's empowering presence in your life. I say this, assuming that you already have asked Jesus to be your Savior and to reign over you.

Right now, you probably feel you have a ton of issues. You feel overwhelmed. You may feel defeated by the way you live. You may be using camouflage to keep people from seeing these parts of your life. Religion is one example of something to hide behind, but another is being socially outgoing or its opposite—being very private; or being indispensable and handy so no one will ask questions; or controlling people and information; or keeping everyone laughing; or putting on a happy face.

But hidden issues will slip out. And if no one else knows, your family does. Moreover, you yourself have a backstage view of yourself. You know the truth. You see no way to fix yourself. The idea that you can become whole seems ridiculous to you.

Discovering the depths of God's love for you is essential to have the courage to go on. Failing to believe this is why you struggle to trust God with your mess.

Perhaps you do find this truth hard to believe. Your inner voice may tell you that God is not all that pleased with you. One person told me that she thought God must be disgusted with her for all the ways she failed to measure up to His standards. You might even think God has it in for you, that He really does not want you to succeed in your life. While I cannot sweep away these lies for you, I can affirm that God's love for you is deeper and more amazing than you can imagine. You will find as you come to know Him better that His love contains the power you need to address your anxiety and fear.

This is why the gospel is *good news*. God has not made His transformation of you dependent on your own puny strength. Out of His love God has given you everything you need to be saved from the power of sin…everything you need to be transformed…everything you need to deal with your unfinished business.

This is not something that God will give you later on when you have become a good person. The power to be transformed was gifted to you from the instant you put your faith in Jesus. Otherwise transformation would be impossible. Peter said this in his second letter. "His divine power has given us *everything we need* for life and godliness through our knowledge of Him who called us by His own glory and goodness. Through these He has given us His very great and precious promises, so that through them you may participate in the divine nature and escape the corruption in the world caused by evil desires" (2 Peter 1:3-4). What is he saying?—that there is nothing you lack to be made whole from the corruption (destructive influences) in the world. You have been empowered through your connection with God in such a complete way that you no longer have to live being damaged and damaging others. This is based on God's promises, not just on Peter's wishful thinking.

What you need to accept is that you have everything you need from God *right now* to be made whole. You do not need to wait for something. You don't have to pray for it. You don't have to pay God back in some way. You don't have to read the Bible more. You don't have to wait for someone to come and lay hands on you. God has already given it to you. The issue is that you must appropriate—mentally grab it and use—what God has already given you.

Since you now know the truth—that you have been given power to be transformed—let me encourage you to continue to explore this process I am describing.

3. SOMEONE WOUNDED YOU

EVERYONE IS WOUNDED

EVERYBODY HAS a back story. A hard charging player on the school football team whose arrogance hides the painful rejection he is experiencing from his dad. His dad thinks he's wasting his time playing sports. He is out to prove that he will be a champion, no matter what his father says.

A loved young teen who spends her days in the grips of deep depression. Who expects the worst to happen because she is being raised in a home full of fear—fear of the future, fear of different people who live in the neighborhood, fear of the end of the world coming.

A guy whose mother was abandoned by his father and left in poverty when he was only ten. Who lacks a positive role model about how to be a man as he grows up. Not hard to see why he might not take school seriously, then quit job after job and seem aimless in life.

A girl who is attracted to violent men because she is being raised in a home where Mom was regularly hit or where household things were smashed against the wall when Dad was drunk.

Your angry friend, who is learning to hold grudges by watching his parents in their ongoing war with his grandparents. The nerdy student who thinks she's dumb because she has been called stupid all her life. The awkward guy who is afraid to make friends because he has been told by his parents that no one will like him because of the way he acts.

How about your back story? It probably wouldn't take a lot of digging to find serious wounds stashed away in some hidden place inside you. Stories that you have marked 'Private' and you plan to keep it that way. Stories that you do not tell to even your closest friends. Stories of hurts you may even have forgotten, but still ache. These stories are not the whole of your life, but they influence how you live your life.

Woundedness is not about temporary hurt feelings that you eventually get over. Nor is it about the pain that discipline inflicts, the 'this-will-hurt-for-a-while' sort given by a parent or mentor that ultimately helps you to become more mature. Woundedness is the gut level kind of pain that not only does not fade, but continues to throb years after the knife was twisted in.

It doesn't matter if your wounds seem minor to anyone else. These wounds are causing *you* pain. You may not even be thinking about them, but when you get around stressful people or into unhappy situations, your wounds determine how you respond.

Wounds are one of the two causes for all your anxiety and fear. I call wounds the *hurt of the heart*, because that's where they go to live. In fact, they are one of the unintended consequences of the Fall of Adam and Eve. As people live out being their own god, making decisions that they feel are good for themselves, their decisions can cause pain to others—and often do. And this goes straight to your heart.

What is the heart? In the Bible, it is considered the place where you make all your life decisions. What you think and what you feel are weighed out so you can make a decision about what you should do and how you will present yourself to others.

Your unfinished business of anxiety and fear keeps your heart from making healthy decisions. It ends up giving you false guidance on how to live your life like a badly mapped GPS. More importantly, your heart is collecting more *hurt of the heart* as you go on through life. Many times they are related and connected wounds. You may bury them inside, but they do not go away on their own.

ORIGIN OF YOUR WOUNDS

Where did all this *hurt of the heart* come from? The answer is—many different sources. Mostly these hurts come from people who are supposed to love and protect you, whose love failed at an important moment. They were not necessarily trying to hurt you. Sometimes they were just doing the best job they could of helping you to become a responsible adult. But their decisions, made so casually, so unthinkingly, may have cut you deeply. The sad part of this is that they often do not even remember wounding you.

This may be hard to admit to anyone, including yourself, but you may be living with your mom's and dad's failure to be good parents. Some are acting unfairly, some are neglectful of your needs, and others are intentionally brutal. You may feel that you are at fault for their divorce or are the cause of their addictions. Some of you are being physically abused. Some are being sexually used by adults that you love. Some of you have been told you are not wanted. Or that you will never measure up to your parents' expectations—or you will always be outshone by your sister's abilities. Or you can't go anywhere because you might get dirty or hurt or lost. Maybe you're told that you are always going to be a failure, a disappointment. Maybe you are growing up in an abusive home, an alcoholic home, with people who are mentally ill. Maybe your parents are workaholics and you never see them. You feel abandoned, or emotionally starved, or mentally abused, or smothered.

And you have not figured out a healthy way to deal with this hurt. These are still issues that you cannot or will not talk about with your parents. You swear when you grow up, you will never be like them. You promise yourself that you will do a better job with how you treat people or make a better choice about your career. Why? Because you think you can fix your pain by trying really hard to be better than them.

It is possible that the most serious wounds you carry do not come from your parents. You may have a great relationship with them. Instead, your trauma is that somebody you were very close to died tragically. Or a friend stabbed you in the back. Or maybe you are being bullied. Or you are the focus of other people's ridicule and contempt. I read about a woman who was beautiful, but could never accept that as true because of being teased about her acne as a teenager. Loss, humiliation, exclusion, and emotional deprivation all leave bleeding wounds in your heart that don't just go away over time.

Here's another category of wounds—those you inflict on yourself. Most of these come from bad decisions due to immaturity. The car crash when you got drunk that cost somebody's life. The bad choice you made to give something away that really meant something to you after all. The wasted school years that will prevent you from pursuing the college you want. The rebellion you live out against the rules that dad and mom set up to help you grow up soundly. The bad personal habits you foster like lying when you are confronted or being late for work which has cost you several jobs. These wounds continue to hang around so that you can beat yourself up over them over and over.

So what can you do? You know you are not happy living with the pain your wounds cause. You may have tried to manage the pain by training your mind not to think about them. By lying to yourself that you do not really hurt, that you have grown up and are now over them. You are numb. You don't care. People do this all the time. But know this—your pain will make its presence felt even while you deny it exists. Remember, something is causing your anxiety and fear and you cannot hide from that something.

You cannot even get rid of it by turning it into something positive. Like helping the homeless. Working a food bank. Being a social justice advocate. Going on a mission trip. Working with handicapped or elderly people. Using your pain to help hurting people. Becoming a counselor or mentor. While all of these activities are noble, they cannot remove the poison of what has stung you.

What you may not understand is the enormous quantity of pain that you are battling. You have not been wounded just once or twice. Your heart is a pin cushion full of tiny painful needles.

Many of them snuck past your defenses to make themselves at home in your soul while you were distracted by other parts of life. Stuff like the challenge of growing up, going through puberty, learning how to work, or to be in a relationship, or maybe even parent a child. Even if you are aware of your hurts of the heart, you probably lack a plan or the energy to work the plan to address all the pain you do know about.

On the other hand, perhaps you are ready to explore your wounds with God. Here's the *ruthless search prayer*. You can say to God, *You have searched me, Lord, and you know me. You know when I sit down and when I get up; you notice my thoughts. You watch me when I go out and when I go to bed. You know everything about me.* (Psalm 139:1-3 paraphrased). *Would you show me where I am damaged so I can be healed by you?*

In asking this, you open yourself up to an epiphany about what is going on inside you. Only God can show you how it makes sense. You are saying to God that you are ready to know what He is willing to show you no matter how scary it is to hear, because you want your soul to be healthy.

AVOIDING VICTIM MENTALITY

Before you explore deeper, ask yourself whether you see yourself as just a victim. After all, there are people responsible for hurting you in ways that were unfair and cruel. Do you choose to see yourself as their victim? What happened was not your fault, you say. And you would be right. What people do to hurt others is never okay. Some of their acts were criminal. As a result of what they did, you may have spent hours and many dollars getting counseling.

The danger is that a lot of counseling encourages you to become a *helpless* victim. The idea is to believe everything that happened in your life was beyond your control, that you just happened to be in the wrong place at the wrong time. It is right to recognize you are a victim of someone's actions you could not control. But deciding you are only a helpless victim with no power will always add to your pain. People who decide they are a helpless victim think they have no role in their continuing pain.

While it is true that people and events have hurt you, you still have a choice about what you are going to do in response to the pain.

Some of you have endured terrible abuse through no fault of your own. You were—or are—someone's sexual prey. Or maybe someone made you his or her personal punching bag. These things are horrible. You did not cause these people to abuse you, to hate you, to rob you of personal dignity and humanity.

No, the issue you have to face is *what are you doing to cope with the wounds*? What did you do once you were wounded? What are you choosing to try to make the pain stop? Are you choosing to continue to define yourself as one who is being used and abused and assume that your life choices are a natural result of trying to survive? Or are you choosing to be strong, yet still in secret the memories ache and the way you are coping is not getting you past the pain?

One person told me how his father deserted his mother when he was a young teen. Having no money or job skills, his mom took them to live with a cold, abusive grandmother. He dealt with the pain by hiding in an internal emotional cave he created. In there he found that no one could bother him and he did not have to answer to anyone. He took this cave with him into his marriage. It ultimately destroyed his relationship because he would run there to hide whenever his wife needed him emotionally.

You may not have an emotional cave to hide in. You choose to be a clown, or a hero, or a perfect child to deal with the abuse you live through. The flaws in that choice now complicate your life as the mature people you need to help you do not see that you need help. They laugh at you or admire you, but you need them to see you instead of the character you are successfully hiding behind.

Accept also that sometimes you contribute to the hurt that haunts you. I once met a young woman who had spent years of her life in depression. As a teen she had fallen for an older man. He privately promised her marriage. As he was many years older, her dad was really against the relationship. To see each other, she would meet secretly with him, sometimes even in her own home when the family was not there. Before long their relationship became physical. But this was okay in her mind because they were going to be married. But then, when she was still a minor, her family moved across the country. Her lover found another bride. She went into a tailspin. It was only years later that she shared with her family the reason for her depression. She saw herself as the victim of this man. She felt she could not move on and pursue a productive life. The family affirmed her victimhood and went looking for his head.

There was no question that the man duped her and drew her into sexual sin. Everything he did ignored her father's order to stay away from his daughter. What was worse was that he denied he had made any promise to her, adding rejection to her pile of pain. In all this she was the victim.

Yet she made decisions that hurt her as well. She chose to believe her lover's promises over her father's protection. She decided to meet him secretly, even in her own home. She freely gave in to sexual acts that she knew to be wrong outside of marriage.

She chose to view herself as only the victim instead of someone who made choices. Instead of her confession helping her to become healthier emotionally, her lack of ownership sent her into a deeper downward spiral. Denying that she had made her own damaging choices kept her stuck for many more years.

Believing your main identity is that you are a victim creates a confusing maze of wrong beliefs about yourself. It tells you that you should be pitied and protected because of your wounds instead of being challenged to examine and take responsibility for the choices you made *after* you got hurt. It encourages you to learn to be helpless—that you are unable to recover until someone rescues you and the person who hurt you is punished.

Being powerless is at the core of victim mentality. You think, "I have no power to get better." So you hide or ignore the pain instead. This is the lie of the enemy that leads you to make terrible choices. And those choices trap you. The truth is, you can make decisions even when you have incredible pain that will lead to becoming a healthier person. You are not stuck with taking what is dished out to you. But the power to become whole—free of anxiety and fear—does not come from within you. You have to surrender to it. I will come back to this later.

What you need to accept right now is that YOU are the only one who stands in your way of getting well. You can choose to not be a victim. You do not have to live the rest of your life with the pain of what people have done to you, said of you, deprived you of. When you decide you no longer want to be a helpless victim, you have taken the first step on the journey to being the person God created you to be.

DAMAGING OUTCOMES

So how do your wounds affect your life? How do they twist your outlook on life and guide your choices?

The direct effect of wounds is that they damage your emotions. Your emotions are one of the two pieces of equipment you use to make life decisions. The second one is your life knowledge, which is about how you think. Making decisions is like putting emotions and thinking on opposite sides of a scale. You weigh these two things out every single time you make a decision.

So what happens when your emotions are damaged? They take on greater weight in the decision making process. Damaged emotions make reality look very different. The result is that, instead of making good, rational decisions, you make irrational ones based on a false reality. You probably do not realize this at the time. Hardly anybody does.

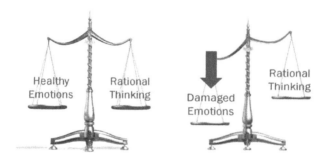

For example, why do you keep eating when you are way overweight and can no longer fit comfortably into your clothes? Your rational mind tries to tell you this is a bad decision, but your damaged emotions override those thoughts, telling you that you need this leftover spaghetti, you deserve this ice cream. Or why do you get mad at other people on the road who are in your way when you are the one speeding? Your rational mind tells you to slow down but your damaged emotions weigh in with the thought that cursing and taking dangerous chances to pass them are better ideas. If you win against people who are not even trying to compete with you, somehow you feel superior.

Or how about the abused teenager whose grandparents took her in to keep her safe, only to have her physically attack them when they did not give her permission to spend the night over at her boyfriend's place. Her irrational thinking turned her from the abused into the abuser. Does this make sense? Not really, but decisions like these are a sure sign your emotions have taken charge of your will.

We even hear people say stupid stuff and to their ears it sounds reasonable. Why do we overspend at sales to buy things we really don't need? To save money! Why do people abuse their friends by playing dirty tricks on them? Because it is funny! Why would I cheat on my girlfriend? Because I am in love! Those damaged-emotion responses seem to explain everything. I once had a friend explain to me that he had to have an illegal radar detector in his car because he could not help speeding. Several times I have sat with people who were thinking about committing suicide and heard them explain how killing themselves would be for the good of their families. The term "rationalization" was coined for this very purpose—we are seeking to make our decisions based on damaged emotions appear to be rational— to make sense—when they are not.

Your damaged emotions always lie to you about what is real. They fill your head with ideas that direct your life down paths where you really won't thrive, but are trapped into going. Thoughts like:

- If I make a mistake, I will never live it down.
- When someone disagrees with my ideas, I am being personally attacked.
- I have to please everyone to be liked.
- What people think of me matters the most.

- If I do not have a boyfriend, girlfriend or spouse, I am a nobody.
- I am failing at life if my plan doesn't work out exactly right.
- Nothing ever goes right for me.
- It's my fault if anything bad happens in my life.
- People are talking about me.

If you find people you trust telling you that your thinking is messed up then you had better pay attention—because you are running your life on your feelings. You may even find yourself using the phrase, "*I feel…*" when evaluating life situations. "*I feel* that no one likes me. *I feel* like running away. *I feel* I am all alone and no one cares about me."

What you need to know at this point is that your wounds have caused this damage to your thinking. Many of the problems you face in life have been influenced by lies going on inside you.

The real problem for you is now you have fear. Now you have anxiety. These inseparable monsters—fear and anxiety—drive you to protect yourself. So you protect yourself from people who love you enough to question your choices. You protect yourself from people seeing the real you. You protect yourself so you will not be damaged further—an impossible task because damage attracts more damage.

If you already have anxiety, guess who you are most likely to turn to for help? —friends who will agree with you.—friends who say you have a right to be anxious.—friends who tell you that you are alright when you're not alright.—friends who will join you in fear and anxiety. And when you discover that someone in your world will not join you in fear and anxiety, you are most likely to end that friendship. Fear teaches you to hide from anyone who might explode the myth that you are okay.

This is how a person gets more damaged as time goes by. Like a faithful watchdog, fear keeps truth at bay. It allows you to avoid seeking real help. It puts a self-protective wall around your ability to mature and grow as a person.

Damaged emotions create one other potential outcome in you. You can get a hard heart towards how God designed life to work. You can find yourself saying "No," to God's ways. You no longer feel God is safe, that God understands your lot in life. Instead, you feel you are better off deciding for yourself what it right and what is wrong.

So you might be kind and thoughtful most of the time, but froth at the mouth when asked to forgive anyone you hold in contempt. Or refuse to rebuild a broken relationship or to surrender your rights instead of getting your way. You might refuse to confess that you were wrong—or even to *see* that you were wrong. Your hard heart will just not let you do so. The hard heart tells you that you are right! The hard heart is self-justified defiance plain and simple.

I saw this in the life of Justin who scared people for fun. Not with pranks that everyone laughed at afterwards. He used terror to evoke fear in those he considered weak so he could feel powerful when he laughed. He would show up wild-eyed, covered with fake blood and bruises to panic a younger teen by saying that a gang of bullies were hunting him to finish him off. The teen was traumatized by Justin's story. Justin was amused. Adults would talk with him about the hurt he was causing and warn him to stop. He ignored them all. As a result, he wounded a lot of people, destroyed people's friendships and ended up friendless.

If you have a hard heart, it is complicating your life. God is the only one who knows how life really works for you. Rejecting God's guidance is always a recipe for more pain, more walls, more anxiety.

Feelings. Fear. Hard Heart. These tell you that you are wounded. As a result, you look at your life through damaged emotions--like a weird filter on your phone--and it messes up the truth. You hear things weirdly, too. Someone gives you a compliment and you immediately think they are probably making fun of you. The health—or sickness--of your soul tells you what you see, what you hear. And it is lying to you with your own voice. This is how damaged you can be.

The worst part of all of this is that the same place you are wounded is where you are love starved. You were created for love. But the wounded part of you will not let you receive it. You deeply want love, but nothing and no one—not your parents, friends, lover, not even your dear aging grandma that spoiled you and fed you special treats as a child—can fill the hole inside you. If you don't know this yet, you will find out it is true in time.

Wounds mark the place where love is needed inside you. But the lie that damaged emotions tells you over and over again is that you are unlovable. So you have set off to find this missing love in all the places that are not God. This is the most devastating aspect of the damage, for we give up on God, who is the source of all love, when God is the answer to our greatest need. And so your heart aches with pain from your wounds, and the Person who is the solution is not recognized as a solution at all.

EMOTIONAL PRESSURE TO FIND RELIEF FROM THE PAIN

We are not made to live with pain. If our head aches, we take aspirin. If it continues to hurt, we go to the doctor, if we can afford one. We could not get by in life if we let a broken arm go without a cast to immobilize it. The physical pain would immobilize us.

It's the same for inner pain. As soon as your emotions start to hurt, you will begin to look for a way to comfort your pain, consciously or unconsciously. You hurt, therefore you eat. Or drink. Or pick fights. Or look at pornography. You come home and watch Netflix or play video games to numb your mind from the pain of the day. You look for an escape. The deeper you hurt, the greater the internal pressure to find comfort. You look for ways to distract yourself from the pain so that you will not have to think about it. Distractions do not heal the pain. The pain will be there when you get back from that shower, your favorite TV show, being with your friends—whatever activity you engage in. And so you will continue to look for the activity that will give you the longest period of relief and the best chance of numbing the pain—hoping in time it will lose its power to hurt you.

This pain will leave you living life in ways you would never choose rationally. What you are doing is running from the pain. This is the normal approach for all people. Since you cannot live with pain, and do not have it in ourselves to block the pain, we see the only path for us is to avoid it through making choices that will comfort that pain. For you to understand the results of these choices in you, you will have to explore what else the Heart Chart shows you about yourself.

The *Hurt of the Heart Inventory for Teens and Young Adults* is
available as a free download at:
www.ChurchEquippers.com/downloadables

4. YOU MADE CHOICES

YOUR ONLY CHOICES ARE ADDICTION OR HEALTH

JORDAN'S SMILE is what first impressed you when you met him. He was bright, polite and radiated potential. Many people who met him took him into their home to help him in life, offering to pay for advanced education for him, giving him paying jobs and offering to be his mentors. For someone who came from a disadvantaged background with no father in the picture, he had people standing in line to fill that role for him.

But it never lasted. He would move in one month and be gone the next, living out of his car. This life started before he was out of high school. He moved out of his family's home for reasons that never made sense to us who met his folks. On top of all this was a growing alcohol/drug addiction which caused him to break out in zombie-like behavior. When the people who were drawn to him got in too close and saw the devastating path he was on, they challenged him to get help, wanted to pay for him to get help. He rejected it all.

And then he was gone. Before he was into his twenties, he was dead. His heart stopped one night, damaged by the lifestyle he lived.

Why did he do this? As I got to know him, I found nothing in his life even hinted he would live out a sad story like this. The family that he rejected actually loved him deeply and wanted him to come home. People were ready to set him up for success in life. He never even stopped going to church weekly, inviting others to go with him. So why did this happen?

The answer is in how he *chose* to comfort the hurt in his heart. Instead of being able to receive love from others, he repelled it. He was starving for love, but what he chose to ease his pain in place of love destroyed him. The outcomes of his inner choices—rejecting family, using an alcohol/drugs combo and running from stability—were not the problem. In the end, his damaging choice of pride and appetite did him in. Keep reading and you will understand what I mean.

WHY PEOPLE MAKE DAMAGING CHOICES

You probably have already made a choice about your pain that is going to be destructive, if it isn't already. This choice was maybe not made consciously. You did not jump on the internet to get it through Amazon. You made this choice because the moment you were wounded in some way, the choice automatically popped up inside you to offer you a way to dull the pain.

You may not be aware that you made a choice. Maybe it's because life is so crazy and painful for you right now. Or maybe you haven't experienced any fallout from your choice yet. So what I said may be a surprise to you. You may think "What is he talking about? I am not on a destructive path." But everyone makes these kinds of choices sometime in their lives, usually in their earliest years. So opting for a destructive choice is not unique to you. This kind of choosing is going on inside every one of your friends, mom, dad, siblings—every person you meet, regardless of where they live, how many advantages they have or lack in life or how smart they are.

So why did you make this kind of choice? It's because you are, well...human. Choices like this are the other unintended consequence of the Fall of Adam and Eve. We already talked about the *hurt of the heart*, but a second something got into our hearts that was never meant to be there, which is *sin in me*, a cancer inside every person alive.

Paul writes about this in Romans 7 when he is explaining his personal confusion about his behavior. Being raised a Jew with a high commitment to keeping the Law of Moses, he confesses that this law is not making him good in the way he wants to be. It's not the Law's fault, he is quick to admit. But when he hears one of the laws read, he immediately wants to do the opposite. It's like seeing a sign to keep off the grass or to not touch the wet paint. Something inside people just wants to do exactly what the sign says not to do.

Paul tells how he is confused by his behavior. In this self-revealing passage, he shares that he does not understand his actions at all. He does things he does not want to do and he doesn't do the good things he longs to do. Even though he knows the right thing to do, he does bad things instead. In fact, God's commands produce a desire in him to rebel against them any way he can, and he can think of a few! His conclusion is, "As it is, it is no longer I myself who do it, but it is sin living in me" (Romans 7:17).

What does he mean by that statement? Paul is using his experience to explain the problem we all have. Though he is a follower of Jesus, the power of sin still has deep roots in his soul. He'll end up declaring what a 'wretched' man he is, meaning that he is miserable—not evil. He is caught between his desire to be good for God and the reality of his life. I am sure you understand this kind of dilemma.

What does *sin in me* mean exactly? Here is where I need to be clear or you will find yourself trying to address the wrong issues. Paul is not speaking about particular actions or attitudes. This may surprise you if you have been brought up to think of sin as a list of forbidden actions. "Don't do this or that." If you keep the rules, you are a good person. If you break the rules, you're a bad person and God will punish you.

What is true is that there is no list of rules that can divide all your life actions into good or evil categories. Some churches try to do this, to make everything black and white. But as Paul explains further in Colossians 3:20-23, giving people rules like, "Do not handle! Do not taste! Do not touch!" may sound spiritually wise, but these rules have no power to fix what is really wrong with anyone. It's like putting lipstick on a pig. The pig might look better, but it still prefers mud.

Sin in me is about what pulls you to the mud. It is about you damaging yourself by following an internal set of motivations which offer you comfort for your pain. These motivations are lying to you. They make you believe you will feel better if you just follow their pull.

The lie is that you can find comfort for your pain somewhere else than God. The entire set of *sin in me* choices harms you, and leaves its hooks in you until you have given up your very life to it—unless you allow God to rescue you. It is the very root of all that destroys you. For that reason, you have to understand the nature of each piece in the set…

THE SEVEN SINS IN ME SET

Seven items to choose from are in this set. Collectively, the set is called the Deadly Sins because they rob you of life. They slowly take over your emotions to the point where you feel dead inside. They kill love for others and make it impossible for you to receive love, which is the essential ingredient of life. You become the walking dead even while you are still alive.

Here is a brief description of each.

Anger: This *sin in me* choice is a way of life for those in its clutches. It has a strong thirst for revenge. It chooses a life full of resentment and bitterness. It argues loudly, fights, or is sullen and silent. It is sarcastic, cynical, insulting, and critical. It counsels frequent irritation and desires harm for others, maybe even physically harming someone. You may regret being violent after anger unleashes it—take for example people who have killed others in a moment of road rage—but at that moment violence feels so satisfying.

Being angry is not always a *sin in me* choice. You can experience good anger. For example, when you see someone bullying another person, or when a person intentionally offends you, God programmed you to feel anger so that you would seek to right that wrong. This is natural and healthy anger.

Anger becomes damaging when it festers inside and motivates you to want to get even. It makes it seem bigger than it was, or sees offence where there is none, or pushes you to live with grudges even when those who have offended us have apologized. As it gets its hooks into us, we find we have no ability to let go of offenses, and they pile up in us like NFL'rs on a loose football.

Appetite: This is about developing a desire for more and more of a certain thing. It triggers an ever-increasing appetite for anything—drugs, alcohol, chocolate, the Internet, food, spending, work—even a person. It takes what is a natural interest or activity in you and intensifies its control over your life. You find that you are no longer satisfied with a natural amount, creating a physical and emotional attachment to needing more. You just cannot get enough!

Giving yourself over to any excessive activity is a signal you are in the grips of appetite. Appetite's poison is that it will direct you to spend everything you've got—money, time, thoughts and strength—trying to satisfy the unquenchable appetite that has been unleashed in you.

Envy: Envy is the green-eyed monster that makes you unhappy with your life. It compares you unfavorably to other people. This *sin in me* choice feeds your discontent over what someone else has, whether a material possession, position, popularity, or success. It breeds unrelenting competition with everyone else. Envy twists you. You find yourself being jealous when even your friend gets a break, secretly glad when that friend suffers a setback. You become discontented with your life, although you may try to hide it.

None of your personal triumphs and abilities will quiet envy when it takes deep root inside you. Even when you have your own achievements to celebrate, you will always be comparing them to other people's accomplishments. This relentless comparison will make you feel you have no value in other people's eyes, but especially in your own eyes.

Greed: If you resist sharing anything you have, greed has its grips on you. Greed is about what you really worship, the true idol of your heart. And because you worship it—money, possessions, getting and keeping wealth—you want more of it than you already have. In fact, you never have enough. You find yourself stockpiling instead of sharing, even with your family members. Furthermore, as greed grows inside you, you feel over-the-top distressed when you suffer even a minor loss.

Greed plays on whatever you need to feel secure. God is your real security—everything you truly need-- but greed says you need to find it somewhere else. This is why you can be convinced that if you can get enough money, you will feel safe. But the number of dollars you need keeps growing in your mind—if you get a thousand you need two thousand, if you get two thousand you need three—so you never really feel safe. On top of that, greed makes you more and more willing to take dangerous risks to find this security—a security that is always just out of reach. You gamble away the money needed to buy food. You might even turn to robbery and theft to 'get your fair share.'

Lust: Lust is about using people to fulfill your sexual fantasies. You exploit others, whether in pictures or in person, for your pleasure, rather than treating them as individuals who have worth. To you, the other person becomes just a tool, like a hammer or screwdriver—

something possessing no feelings—that you use for a specific purpose and then put away. In other words, when you are motivated by lust you want a possession, not the person, to satisfy your desires. The reverse is also true. Lust will dull your self-worth until you live life just to be an object of desire in the eyes of others.

No long-term bond is built on lust, no matter how long the relationship lasts. Any love that may have existed between two people is lost when they are in the grips of lust, because lust is ultimately about one's personal gratification and not about deep partnership built on intimacy.

Sloth: This is the most misunderstood *sin in me* choice of the seven. Sloth sin is not just about being lazy. If you are caught up in sloth, you are really struggling with the unwillingness to take responsibility for yourself. Sloth will lead you away from what is necessary for your growth and health. "I can't change." and "It is not my fault." or "It's someone else's responsibility." are phrases used by people in the grips of sloth. Only doing the part of your schoolwork that you like and avoiding the rest is a sloth decision. Living in a pigpen room is sloth at work in you. Having to be constantly rescued by your parents from bad decisions is a sign of sloth.

You might be surprised about the emotional impact of those dominated by sloth. Some of the most common symptoms are sadness, feelings of helplessnes, habitual procrastination, boredom, restlessness, and preoccupation with activities that have no value. Many people who make sloth choices end up suffering from ongoing depression. Suicide can be an end product of sloth. The reason why is that sloth robs people of the feelings of self-worth and self-respect. As they lose the healthy sense of responsibility for their lives, hopelessness that life will never be better develops, especially since they lack the inner drive to own and influence their life's outcome.

Pride: The last piece in the set is ultimately about believing you are the center of your world. Secretly you believe you really ought to be in control of everything because you could run things so much better. It shows arrogance, an attitude of being superior to others. It is self-satisfied, anxious to get credit, desires to occupy the first place, is strongly opinionated, inflexible, and is unwilling to submit to authority and the rule of God.

Pride does so much to define your life, but you probably do not see how much it influences you. It paints a rosy picture of what you are, allowing you to hold a higher opinion of yourself than you should. Even if you think you hate yourself—calling yourself a failure or some other nasty name—pride still keeps you away from dealing with your problems in a healthy way. How? By making it nearly impossible to see that you have faults or need help.

If you could step away from your pride, you might see the humor in everyone in the world sharing this same I-am-the-center-of-the-universe belief. Perhaps we need to be reminded that the point of the creation of the world was not to bring us personally into existence! But for many, this is no laughing matter. People are seriously dominated by their own overinflated view of their worth. So are you. So am I.

A *Deadly Sin Inventory for Teens and Young Adults* to help you examine privately for yourself how the deadly sins are affecting your life is available as a free download for you at: www.ChurchEquippers.com/downloadables

THE FALSE COMFORT OF DEADLY SIN

Go back now to your *hurt of the heart*. The result of hurt is that your emotions are damaged. You do not want to feel pain. So what does the *sin in me* do? It offers you a way to comfort your pain by suggesting, "Here is a way you can deal with any wounds in your life so that you don't have to feel the pain."

This is how *sin in me* lies to you. It deceives you into believing that you can feel better without ever having to deal with your *hurt of the heart*. After all, you hurt already and do not want to add to your misery by facing this pain. So you choose to run from the pain and believe the *sin in me*'s lie—let the pain take care of itself while you are distracted by the *sin in me*.

This is how you get hooked on any of the *sin in me* choices you make. Each *sin in me* choice has an emotional factor. It offers you a feeling that blocks the source of your *hurt of the heart*. So when you made your choice, the hurt and sin bonded together, forming a deep connection. Both now work in lockstep—I hurt, sin comforts. I hurt again, sin comforts again. *Sin in me* just keeps showing up like an unwanted pop up ad on your favorite website.

Instead of your pain, now you feel empowered by anger, you enjoy the sensuality of lust, and you experience the easy-goingness of sloth, or perhaps the numbing impact of feeding an appetite. These emotional narcotics pull you along and mask the fact that you are still hurt. Your comfort choice now has you on emotional steroids. In the short run, you do feel better and you like it.

For example, take the guy who has been made to feel that he is not a man by his parents. What *sin in me* could he choose to comfort himself? Different options are open to him. Lust might lead him to sleep with lot of girls to convince himself that he is a man. Or he might use anger to dominate others, letting him feel like a man. Or pride might propel him into competing and achieving in high school to prove to his unseeing parent that he is really a man. If his parents' attitude awakens a sense of failure in him, he might indulge in the spite of envy towards someone who is more the man he wished he was. Or he might just give up and prove he isn't a man by living a life of sloth. Or choose appetite and use drugs, alcohol, overeating, or spend lots time playing video games—anything that will comfort him so that he will not feel the pain of not being thought of as a man. And he will go on to build a lifestyle around whatever he chooses. His preferred *sin in me* will mark him as long as he allows it to be his comfort for the *hurt of the heart.* This is not the same as *dealing with* the pain of feeling he is not a man.

Or a woman feels pain because people question her looks. "How you look matters!" is a message that's communicated to many girls early in their lives. In the smorgasbord of various comfort options, a woman might choose anger and become bitter towards those who she thinks feel superior in some way to her. Or she may select lust and seek to present herself as the object of desire to guys, using sex to gain a sense of personal attractiveness. Or she may give herself over to appetite choices and gain a lot of weight to fend off attention from guys to save herself from expected rejection. Or she may prefer envy and be unable to befriend other women whom she thinks have what she lacks. Each choice can dull the pain, even if the outcome destroys her life.

These comfort choices may be unconsciously made, but they tragically illustrate how we become what we don't want to be. I do not know anyone who wanted to be a train wreck, who wanted to have an unhappy life. But a lot of people live with anxiety and fear and do not know why. What you just read about deadly sin is the reason.

Even worse, you do not have just one pain for the *sin in me* to exploit. You have multiple wounds inside you that you are comforting with deadly sin. The longer you live, the more *hurt of the heart* issues you are accumulating and the more *sin in me* choices you are making. This means you probably are comforting a multitude of unrelated hurts with one or more of the seven *sin in me* choices. This interweaving of hurt issues complicates your ability to become whole again.

What you choose depends on what draws you. Specific *sin in me* choices may be more attractive to you because you see them daily at home. If you are drawn to greed, chances are that greed goes back generations in your family tree. If you feed an appetite—say in the form of alcoholism—you may have been influenced towards this first at home. I once helped a guy trace anger in his family tree. He was able to remember serious anger stories of his father, grandfather, and his great grandfather—three generations back. It gave him greater insight into his own choices.

However, your *sin in me* choices are not limited to what may be happening at home. Your choices reflect the damaging impact of the Fall of Adam and Eve on your personal makeup. You choose your damaging *sin in me* choice because it clicks with the way you find comfort. Because you made these choices unconsciously at first, you really have no idea why you chose what you did. So don't blame your family. Your family is not responsible for your choices no matter how they live their lives. Admit to yourself that you are the one who did the choosing if you want to go on to freedom and health. We'll cover more on this later.

WHERE YOU GO FROM HERE

If you accept the truth of what I just shared, you might believe you now know enough to alter your choices. You might feel you can now make changes. If you think this, you will probably be disappointed because understanding about *sin in me* choices is not enough. The anxiety and fear—unfinished business—you are struggling with goes deep. Since—not *if*—you have made choices about comforting your hurts, you must understand two other issues that come into play.

First, your *sin in me* choices have led you to addiction. What started out giving you comfort has taken firm root inside you, so that you no longer are choosing *sin in me* but now are being controlled by it. The outward symptoms of your inner choices have gained a stranglehold on you, stubbornly holding on against every determined attempt by you, or those who love you, to overcome them.

Second, you lack the personal power to change yourself. To address something as controlling as the *sin in me*, you will need transformational power (being changed to be like Jesus by the Spirit), not reformational power (trying to change yourself to look like Jesus). I illustrate this to those I work with in this way:

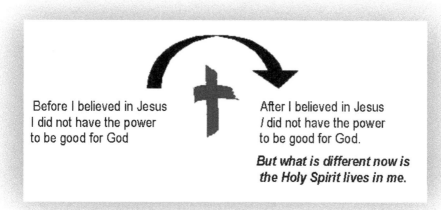

Before I believed in Jesus
I did not have the power
to be good for God

After I believed in Jesus
I did not have the power
to be good for God.

*But what is different now is
the Holy Spirit lives in me.*

Trying to change in your own power is an illusion. You may find yourself trying to find a happy place away from fear and anxiety or playing pretend to shove down the urges, trying hard to be obediently different, but not really getting better. The good news is that the power to be transformed is already present now in you. I will come back and tackle the issue of transformational power further after I explain some other important stuff.

5. UNEXPECTED CONSEQUENCES

WHAT IS WRONG WITH ME

"WHAT'S WRONG with me?" The answer is that your unfinished business is outwardly messing up your life, increasing your pain. In fact, as your life goes on with unaddressed inward issues, your unfinished business will progress from being a pesky nuisance to a full blown intruder which takes you over and trashes your hopes. Its anxiety and fear will also mark you in ways you didn't see coming.

A number of years after I left home, my mom called me to tearfully apologize. She had been watching old home movies and had come across a scene where I was being cruelly teased when I was three years old. It struck her deeply, remembering how I had gone from being a smiling little boy to being sullen-faced all the way through my teen years. She knew that this was, in part, because of the wounds that she and other family members had casually inflicted on me.

I remember hanging up and puzzling over her apology. Was I sullen-faced still? I didn't want to think I was, but the mirror I stared into did not lie. I discovered that this and other wounds, comforted by my unconscious *sin in me* choices, had left its mark on not just my face, but my behavior as well.

You have outward marks on you. These outward marks are what I call symptoms. Symptoms are produced when your *sin in me* choices bond with your hurt of the heart. Again, the symptoms (like the stuffy nose in the first chapter) are not the real problem, but others often view these symptoms as what is wrong with you. That's because the symptoms are out there where everyone in your world can see them.

They can feel natural and normal to you, yet still be robbing you of joy, friendship, peace and love. You find yourself thinking and acting in broken ways you come to enjoy, even believing you are empowered by them. Some of them get you sympathy. Some cause people to avoid you or laugh at you or handle you with heat-resistant gloves. These symptoms wake you up in the night and show up in the arguments you have with your family—and former friends.

There are all kinds of symptoms, but the guiding definition for all of them is this: whatever you do or think that is not in keeping with the character of Jesus. Now, if you have never really studied the gospels in the Bible—Matthew, Mark, Luke and John—that last statement may not make much sense to you. But it is an important one.

You see, in Romans 8:29, God tells us what His plan is for everyone who puts their faith in Jesus. "God knew what he was doing from the very beginning. He decided from the outset to shape the lives of those who love him along the same lines as the life of his Son. The Son stands first in the line of humanity he restored. We see the original and intended shape of our lives there in him." is how the Message Bible puts it. Paul says that God had already decided before you, me or anyone else became a believer that He would change us to become like Jesus. This is the good news of the gospel—we do not have to continue to be messed up, full of anxiety and fear. Instead, God, who loves us with an unbreakable love, has a better life for us that He will make happen by His power.

Since your life is going to be shaped by God—transformed—so you look like Jesus, then you need to know what kind of person Jesus was. How did he relate to his Father? What did he do? How did he treat people? What was important to him? The point of knowing this is not so you can *try* to be like Jesus. It is so you will know what God is going to do in you. We'll see more of this in the next chapter.

For the moment, the pressing issue is what behaviors and attitudes do you have in your life that you never see in Jesus? You may be aware of a whole truckload of these. Your list depresses you because you realize how messed up you are. Or you might be totally puzzled by the question. After all, you may be someone who has gone to church all your life and feel pretty good about your life and your actions. Nothing comes to mind that you think should be addressed.

But you are still anxious and fearful. And that is why you need to look more closely at Jesus to discover what symptoms are marking you. As I said in the beginning, they are not your problem, but they do indicate that something is wrong with you.

SEEING YOUR SYMPTOMS

One of two useful questions for people who want to change is, "Where is that symptom coming from?" Once you see a symptom in yourself, you can look for its roots. What caused your wounds? What *sin in me* choices did you make? Seeing symptoms can help you know what you need to surrender to God for healing and freedom.

Self-protection holds people back from actually exploring this question. Admitting that you are a mess, that there is something wrong inside you can feel like a self-betrayal. So instead of being honest with yourself, you try to explain/ why you are really all right—why exploring your symptoms is a waste of time—why everybody else has symptoms (some worse than yours), too!

None of these self-protective excuses will set you free from anxiety and fear. This kind of step takes ruthless honesty with yourself. Ruthless honesty is the kind that says I am willing to look at the worst aspect of myself if it will bring me freedom. The way to freedom may be to face the pain, but I am willing because I will not be doing this alone. God is in this with me.

If you are ready to answer this first question, here is a list of symptom categories that offer you some insight into what is damaging to your life. You probably won't see something in you from every category. Just look for the things in you that are not in keeping with the character of Jesus.

- **Stuff you hide.** These symptoms are either embarrassing to you or would make you a social outcast if others knew. You choose to do these behind closed doors and hide them even from your friends and family. You plan times when you can do it so that no one will know.
- **Stuff you used to apologize for.** You have a way with words that come out of your mouth and you regularly choose actions that stomp all over other people's feelings. We used to call these things "rude, crude and socially unacceptable." But you may have been practicing them so long that you have stopped apologizing and don't care what anyone thinks.
- **Stuff that irritates you in others.** Harsh judgment you make about what others do is probably revealing what is wrong with you. If something others are doing—how they treat their boyfriend or girlfriend, act up in class, think about politics, etc., bothers you, it may be that you are doing—or want to do—what they are doing but never can admit it.

- **Stuff causing you pain.** You know you are going to hate yourself but here you go again. You knew you would be found out if you did it one more time, and you were right. You did these things with your eyes open and now the hurting has started again—physically, mentally, or emotionally.

- **Stuff that breaks relationships.** You have left a trail of broken friendships. People no longer call you and block your text messages. And it is because of that thing you do and have defended as being okay for you to do. Except you are now lonely and feeling alienated from the ones that mattered to you at one time. If you honestly trace these broken relationships back to yourself (after all, you are what all these broken relationships have in common), you can discover behaviors in you that were the beginning of the end of those friendships.

- **Stuff that wounds others.** From the people who have not left your life or even people who you come into casual contact with—for example a fast food server, the mall guard, a neighbor up the street—you are getting an 'ouch' reaction. Some of them roll their eyes when they see you coming. You have not yet heard their nicknames for you, but the names are not pretty. What are you doing or saying that is causing the ouch?

- **Stuff that increasingly costs you more and more resources.** What you used to love in moderation now is robbing you like a thief. More and more of your time, thoughts and money is becoming wrapped up in maintaining your pet behaviors. (*This could include too much video gaming or stuffing your closets with overpriced clothes you rarely wear.*)

- **Stuff that you cannot stop doing.** You promised yourself "This will be the last time" the last time you did it, but here you are at it again. These symptoms are set off by the obsessive/compulsive button in you. Many of these started out as good things to do or be but now are lived out like an extreme sport. You find you cannot live without them.

- **Stuff that you cannot see in yourself.** This may sound like an impossible category to assess, but actually it is quite simple. All you have to do is remember the comments you have received from loving friends, teachers and family who have risked offending you by mentioning some damaging behavior or attitude in you. You can't see it. But they told you for your own good. What symptoms did they point out to you?

Why bother with this inventory (in case you are planning to skip it)? The reason you want to is because whatever symptoms you have, they have the potential to become much worse—and you might be already living with that worse. Not just some of your symptoms—all of them are equal in their capacity to damage you. The symptom you choose not to see may become your master and you its slave.

WHY WE DO NOT JUST QUIT

You might think that you will just chuck your symptoms when you become aware of them. Here are three reasons why you probably won't just quit.

The first reason is that your relationship with God probably lacks depth. You may go to church regularly and recite all the right beliefs. You may even have a good grasp of what is in the Bible. But the flaw revealed in humankind when Adam and Eve chose to rebel is our desire to blame God for our mess. "It's your fault God that I got this woman!" was Adam's accusation against God. And we all secretly—or not so secretly—say something like this: "It's your fault God that I was bullied, that I was not kept safe, that I have such difficult parents, _____ (fill in your own rant)." Instead of seeing God's love for you, you see the harm that has come to you from living in the world He should be doing a better job of running!

This gets in the way of wanting to pursue intimacy with Him. You pull away from Him and wonder why He demands—or why His church demands—so much of you. You get angry at Him for not stopping the pain, maybe while you deny that you are angry. I have friends who even stop believing there is a God at all. The point is, it's hard to ask God to heal you when, at some level, you are blaming Him for your anxiety and fear.

The second reason is the role modeling you have received from parents and other adults. One guy I know had a dad who regularly beat up the mom. He tried to protect his mother, and had told himself he would never be like that when he grew up. Until he got his own girlfriend and began slamming her around—ending that relationship in a hurry. And the ones that followed turned out the same. But violent parents breed violent offspring. The ones lied to become liars. The sexually abused are the next generation abusers.

Unthinkingly you inwardly absorb the actions and attitudes of the adults in your life, even though you may believe what they do is awful. You end up living your life the same way, choose the same sin to comfort yourself and find you cannot escape your role models. What is more is that you are often very comfortable being just like them.

The third reason is how easily you fall for the lies of Satan. When you find yourself out of step with God, truth has a way of becoming twisted and sounding hollow. Satan shows up with his pretty lies. He speaks to your bruised ego. He sympathizes over your wounds. He suggests a way of hopeful recovery. Satan lies to you every day, until his lies begin to take on the appearance of reality and you give in to his suggestion to try sin just this once.

Except it never is just this once. *All sin is addictive.* READ THAT AGAIN! Do you understand what this means? It means that in a very short time the sin you choose will take charge of your will and you will no longer be able to choose not to do it. Your damaged emotions will press you to do it again and again until you give in. You will not be able to stop yourself. And in time you will learn to live with it. That kind of addiction will happen to anyone who buys into Satan's lies.

SYMPTOMS BECOME ADDICTIONS

Everyone you know has symptoms. Most of them are doing their best to keep them from messing up their lives. Like a person who is angry inside. She may try to not let that anger loose when it means not getting to use the family's car. Or he might want to keep it under control so he won't get kicked out of class again. Or a person in the grips of greed might realize that having friends involves sharing the costs of going out together. Or the slothful guy who knows he has to at least wash and clean out his car if the love of his life is going to go out in it with him.

But life is full of stress. Not every minute, but when stress comes, it can be like a tsunami. It upends your settled life with its own version of emotional trauma. This trauma puts added pressure on all the wounds you carry inside. What happens next is you start medicating yourself by letting go of one or more of your symptoms. You use them for all their worth to fend off the emotional trauma of stress. This is the moment when you will cross the line from symptom to addiction.

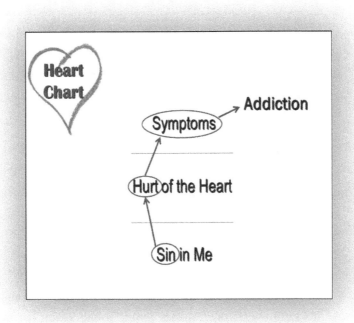

You may be confused about the word 'addiction.' You probably associate it with drug users or alcoholics. Certainly they are addicts. But just because you are fortunate not to have those kinds of addictions does not mean your life is not controlled by something just as damaging. In fact, like everyone else you are driven by forces you do not even notice because their addictive nature is as much a part of your life's fabric as breathing.

One person I know has theft addiction. She stole stuff from every place she ever worked—until she got caught and fired. She even stole from her family, but she could not tell you why. She said she didn't need any of the things she took. She hated how her stealing caused friends and family to turn against her. But she could not resist its destructive control over her.

This is the irony of choosing sin for comfort. You are wounded and choose to comfort yourself with one of the deadly sins. Now you are addicted to that *sin in me* choice. As a result, you are wounding yourself—losing friends, respect, independence, health, a spot on the team, opportunities, money you cannot afford to spend. You lose your way. You watch your best friends avoid you. Your body or your mind breaks down. Most of all, you lose your peace of mind. This is where anxiety and fear make their presence felt in your life.

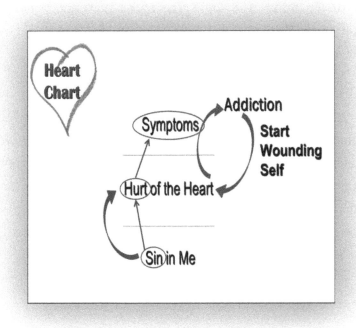

Like one guy I knew who girls rejected because he pressured them for sex on the first date. Underneath his playboy persona was a very lonely person. But he confused love with lust. It became the *sin in me* go-to-choice for every dating relationship. In time, it owned him, dancing on the grave of his dashed hopes of finding someone to love him.

Nothing inside you can stop your addictions from ruining your life. Once they have power over you, you can no more easily shed them than you can shed your skin. You don't have the power to free yourself. Your *sin in me* choice is no longer about comforting your pain. It's about killing the person you were meant to be. The lie of the enemy always leads to death. Addiction is part of that journey to death.

When I was a teen, I worked for a few weeks with a young guy named Jose on an electrical job. He had been an alcoholic since middle school. After numerous rounds of rehab, fresh starts and boozing again, his parents had had enough. As he was now eighteen, he was thrown out to make it on his own—sink or swim.

But the alcohol had damaged his brain. Every day, we retaught him how to wire a plug or switch all over again. He just could not retain what he learned. The last frustrating day before he disappeared from my life, he looked at us in despair and asked, "What's wrong with me?" He was not merely talking about his failure to retain information. His whole life was misery, with no one to love him, to guide him, to give him a hand up. And worst of all, he could not stop himself from giving in to the addiction that had robbed him of so much.

You may be on your way to living out a similar story. Not just addiction you might consider bad for you, such as beating up people or bullying or saying hateful things about someone of a different cultural background or prostituting yourself. Normal life activities can become distorted by using them for comfort. You can become addicted to food, sex, leisure, education, relationships, work—anything that is touched by your *sin in me* choices. Why can't some people pass up a handful of cookies or two or three even after their weight has ballooned to obesity? Why has Internet pornography become such a problem? This is just a sampling of uncomfortable questions. The scope of addiction is so broad that a complete listing of potentially addictive activities is impossible.

If you continue in your addiction long enough, you can go into a death spiral, finding yourself in a place you never wanted to go. You essentially come to the pit of despair and jump in willingly with your eyes open. That is when your normal life, as you know it, comes totally apart. I call this going into the death spiral.

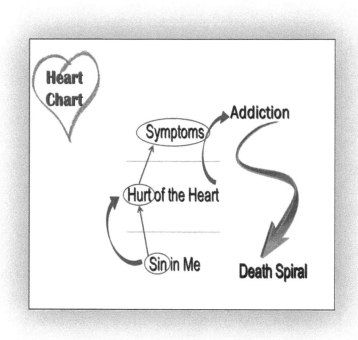

There are two truths you have to accept about addiction if you are going to find freedom. The first is that addiction is powerful; much more powerful than you. You will not be able to stop on your own, no matter how hard you try. Your mind can see where the addiction is leading you, but you cannot stop doing it, even if you are on the brink of death. That's how powerful addiction is. If you will not accept this truth, you will not turn to God for your rescue.

The second truth is that you really enjoy what you are addicted to. No use lying to yourself. You look at pornography because you like to see naked people. You get even with those who hurt you and love it. You revel in overeating—you cannot have too much ice cream! Your road rage is justified, and do you ever feel justified. There is always tomorrow to find a job, so enjoy your movie marathon today with no guilt. Whatever your addiction, you do it again and again because you enjoy it, even though it is leading you to destruction. Admitting you like doing what is destructive to you is honest and opens the door for a real relationship with God.

NEEDING JESUS TO DELIVER AND HEAL

Your story does not have to end in despair and destruction. You can choose even now to surrender to Jesus, who alone is able to overcome your addiction through two powerful actions. The first is for Jesus as the king who reigns over you to deliver you from the *sin in me*. That is why God sent Jesus into the world in the first place. Sin not only broke your relationship with Him, but causes damage in you that only He can repair.

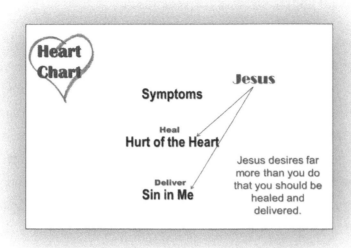

Yielding to Jesus' reign over the *sin in me* is not enough, however. To break from the power of sin, we also need Jesus as the Great Physician to heal the *hurt of the heart*. Healing is the necessity for our souls. If we do not allow Jesus to touch the hurt, closing ourselves off to His examination and prescription, then we are doomed to repeat the cycle of hurt, comfort and addiction for as long as we resist. You see, we cannot live with hurt. We naturally look for ways to stop the pain. If we say to Jesus that He can reign over the particular motivational sin that for years we have used to soothe the *hurt of the heart*, another of the remaining six will offer comfort in its place. A new addiction will appear out of this choice, different from the first one, but in time just as damaging.

This is the point where many people stop. As mentioned before, our wounds really do hurt. We would rather God not go there and touch them because of how badly they hurt. Let me encourage you not to choose to stop but to go on. Courageously risk something with Jesus instead of putting off healing. If you do not, addiction will rule your life again in time.

If this is making some sense to you, you may think you are ready to become whole again. If so, there is a question you have to face…

6. DO YOU WANT TO GET WELL?

YOU HAVE TO ANSWER THIS QUESTION

ONE OF MY FRIENDS talks about how he was regularly beaten and abused by his dad as a very young boy. Every night he asked God to take away his pain and he slept peacefully. Today he is a whole, healthy, and kind person, especially towards his own children.

You may feel you are in a hopeless situation. You may be alone and confused and feel that there is no one to help you.

You may still be at home where you are being hurt regularly. Or maybe it's a situation at school or people who live in your neighborhood that make your life miserable. Right now there is no escape, no place to hide where you will not be found and brought back. You may think that you have no choices but one—to just survive. That kind of thinking is going to do you more damage than the emotional slams you are receiving at the moment. You will grow up to be trapped by your own mind.

Or maybe you have moved out to a place where you hope to be safe. But the wounds that you collected moved out with you—inside you. They will not go away with distance or time.

I'm telling you right now that there is hope. God is with you. He has not abandoned you. He can free you of your anxiety and fear even while you are in the middle of a terrible life situation. He is your strongest ally and is able to release you from the power of addictive sin.

You can choose differently even now, even if you still live with unsafe people. You can choose healing instead. And being healed will depend on how you respond to Jesus' question.

In John 5, Jesus spies a man by the pool of Bethesda who had been stuck there for thirty-eight years waiting for a miracle. People believed that an angel came and stirred the pool every now and then. They thought the first sick person to get into the disturbed water would be healed. Jesus' question to him was, "Do you want to get well?" What Jesus meant was, "Do you want to live a healthy life or have you decided to live out the rest of your life as the old sick guy at the Bethesda pool?"

You may think when you first read the story that the guy's answer is obvious. Who wouldn't want to get well after being sick so long? But people are much more complicated. Often people have gotten used to the way they are 'sick.' Attracting sympathy or getting attention or putting up a wall to keep people out by your sickness can be far more important to you than getting well.

This guy certainly had a lot at stake. Every day someone got him up, fed and dressed him and carried him to the pool—and then collected him again every night. If he got well, he would have to get a job and take care of himself. He wouldn't have time to see all his friends by the pool. And who knew what kinds of obstacles he would face trying to establish himself in the world at such an advanced age. At least at the pool he had a life he could understand, even if it stunk. Saying 'Yes' to the question would cost him.

Jesus is asking you this same question. Do you want to get well? Understand that saying 'Yes' will cost you something. Saying 'Yes' may cost you friends who love the person who your unfinished business has made you. It may cost you an identity you have worked hard to maintain. It may shake up your family, trigger deep emotions about past events, or compel you to give up things you did not plan on losing. As Jesus taught in one of his parable, 'count the cost' before you decide how to answer this question.

But weigh your answer against the fact that there is no other way to rid yourself of your unfinished business and shed your anxiety and fears. To get well, you have to say 'Yes' to Jesus' question. There is no middle ground—no 'Maybe.' Your answer either opens or closes the door to the healing process which frees you to be made whole.

RISKING IT ALL WITH JESUS

The Bethesda pool guy confirmed he was interested in getting well, but he had never been first into the pool. He had tried over and over again to get in when the angel stirred it, but failed. More importantly, he never had anyone to help him be first. It's just the reality he lived with year after year as long as he could remember.

You may feel you are alone in your situation. You think you have no one to turn to for help, no one who seems to understand, no one who you really trust. And it is not like you haven't asked for help at times. You have put out feelers, hoping that someone—a friend, a teacher, a pastor—will help you to get healthy.

So you have tried the best you're able to put yourself back together. And what you have found is that your strength is too puny to maintain any forward progress. It's been one step forward – three steps back. Sometimes it was because you found life too complicated. Sometimes you have sabotaged yourself, deliberately going back into the behavior or relationship or situation that you originally were trying to escape.

The question Jesus asks is an empowering one. If you say 'Yes,' then you will discover he is the person you have been looking for to help you. Because he is not only asking, he is ready to set you free from the anxiety and fears that trap you, that keep you by your own pool of Bethesda. What you must decide is whether or not you are willing to risk everything with Jesus.

Jesus was the person for whom the man had been waiting for thirty eight years to help him. All the man had to do, Jesus said, was pick up his mat and he would be able to walk. Picking up his mat was the real test of whether he really meant 'Yes.' Just saying 'Yes' does not necessarily mean you really want to get well. You might like the idea of getting well or think "Why not give it a shot?" But actually responding to the invitation—making a move—can be daunting, with your emotions screaming at you "No, no, no, no, no! Don't go there!"

And this was not a good picking-up-your-mat day for the man. It was a Sabbath. In Jesus' time, picking up and carrying your mat on a Sabbath day meant that you were breaking a sacred law. People could literally stone you to death for such an act. The pool of Bethesda was in a very public area, so this man had no way to slip home quietly unobserved. It was a dangerous choice.

I can tell you from my own journey that taking this risk with Jesus does not mean it will be an easy ride. I had tried all the anger management tricks. I had apologized multiple times when I stepped over the line. I cannot tell you how many times my anger publically embarrassed me. But when I seriously took Jesus' invitation to pick up my mat—and it was a deliberate choice of saying 'Yes'—the process he took me through was painful. He stripped away my defenses and showed me the hurt I had been comforting with anger. This was much harder and more humbling, yet more freeing that anything I had experienced trying to get well by myself.

With Jesus, you do not have to be afraid of facing the pain. He is here to make you well. Sometimes this is hard to believe. One young guy I guided in this process told me about the multiple wounds he had experienced. But he just could not bring himself to speak openly about the sexual abuse he had suffered at the hands of a family friend. It filled him with shame. Frankly, he would rather have been stoned by a howling crowd than to say it out loud. But the day came when he decided he wanted Jesus to make him well more than he wanted to lay by the pool. He cried as he shared it with me (Jesus had already cried for him long before that day)—and *he got well*.

WHAT YOU WANT TO KNOW

If you decide to say 'Yes' to Jesus' question, what then? Here are three lessons I learned on my journey that will help you understand what is keeping you by your personal pool of Bethesda.

Be willing to learn what you don't know about yourself from God.

Your journey to wholeness should start with asking God to show you what you do not know about yourself. Often people think they know what their wounds are. They point to someone doing or saying something to them at a particular time that caused their pain. Let me warn you not to be fooled by what seems to be obvious.

If you have siblings, you might realize that they had some of the same hurtful experiences you did, but may not share your same pain. This is true because we all process life in different ways. People close to you can be bullied or lied to or manipulated or emotionally neglected just like you were, and internally interpret the event differently. You might see it as harm while they see it as love or ignorance or a personal growth opportunity. Yet even if it did not hurt your brother or sister in the same way, it still was something wrong that happened to you and there's no shame in saying it hurt you.

You are an individual. What you want to know is: How has this hurt shaped how I think about myself? Does it make me feel unloved or useless or alienated or damaged? Do I believe I'm worthless, hopeless, or powerless? Am I insignificant or do I feel entitled? All these are ways people interpret the pain inside them.

How can you know? If you honestly want God to bring about deep change in you, the starting point is to openly ask Him to do a ruthless search. I am talking again about King David's prayer in Psalm 139: "Search me, O God, and know my heart; test me and know my anxious thoughts. Point out anything in me that offends you, and lead me along the path of everlasting life." What you are asking God to do is to show you what He alone knows about you—your faulty way of making decisions, your anxiety, stuff that has set you on the wrong path of life.

The search is ruthless not because God is harsh, but because He is thorough. He opens your eyes to see what you cannot see about yourself. We tend to want to go easy on ourselves. I know I did. During my college days, I had a job that gave me access to the key that opened the snack machine. To be blunt, I stole snacks. As time went by, I stole more and more. I told myself that it was okay, that I worked hard for the company and deserved them, that I needed these snacks—free, of course—because I had to work over my dinner time. And so I stole with my own permission, never even feeling faintly wrong, until God searched me—and guided me to pay it all back.

God knows. He has always known. And He is willing to show you, if you are ready to know.

This kind of knowledge ultimately is about facing the deepest truths about yourself in light of a real relationship with Jesus. Understanding what God's search reveals about yourself does not involve going to church more often or offering to do more things for God.

What happens is you wake up and discover that you are really with Jesus. That he is not just some ideal that people talk about at church, but a living person who cares about you. And you find you are willing to let him change you.

It's like the time Jesus talked with the five-times-married-and-now-living-with-another-man woman at the well in John 4. As they spar together over his offer to give her living water and she pushes back with her questions of his sanity, it slowly dawns on her that Jesus was someone more than some passing Jew looking for a drink of water. He was more than a debater of truth. He did not care to prove his superiority, but cared about what she had become. She runs back to her fellow villagers with the news, "This man told me everything I ever did!" Clearly she was amazed he did not reject her. I am certain John included her story because she was never the same messed up person thereafter.

Jesus plans the same for you. The good news of Jesus' gospel is he is going to restore you into the person you were created to be. It may be hard for you to believe because of your unfinished business. But you are not alone now—Jesus is glued to your side. The kind of relationship with Jesus is different because you do not need to fake anything with him. He knows you and is not put off by the flaws and damage that are currently defacing your life.

Be willing to acknowledge the choice you made to put yourself by the pool.

The second lesson I learned was to acknowledge my choices. I freely chose anger and other deadly sins for comfort. No one forced me to make those choices. No one held a gun to my head to make me choose sin. I chose sin's comfort because *I wanted to*.

You did not cause the wounds that hurt inside you. You did not cause your parent's divorce. You did not choose to be abused, bullied or betrayed. You had no control over the sinful decisions of the people who casually or uncaringly hurt you.

But you did make the *sin in me* choice to comfort your pain. This is why you are still stuck by the pool. The way to health is taking responsibility for your choice. You will need to say to Jesus, "I did choose _____ and it made my life worse instead of better. I am responsible for the life I chose to live, not the people who hurt me (*they don't know and may not even care that you are stuck*). I don't just want you to heal my hurt. I need you to deliver me from the power of this sin."

You see, getting well is more than just not wanting to be sick anymore. It is a positive choice to trust that Jesus can make you whole—choosing that you are ready to abandon *sin in me* as the way to comfort yourself. This is impossible for you to do on your own.

This was a painful lesson for me to learn. I flirted with getting well for a long time, but kept falling back into blaming my parents for why I was so messed up inside. I actually scared my girlfriend (now my wife) one day with a total emotional meltdown over never being able to be the person I wished I could. Then I would revert back to trying to act like someone who had it together and doing everything I thought was expected of me as an emerging adult. Back and forth I'd go—stable one day and using *sin in me* to comfort myself the next. I was stuck by the pool of Bethesda, until I finally confessed I was there because I chose to be there.

This is what sin does to you. It can keep you trapped and pull you right back into a worse version of the anxiety and fears you thought you escaped. So tell the truth to yourself and to God. "I am damaged because I chose sin to comfort my wounds instead of coming to you for healing."

BE READY TO RECEIVE FROM GOD WHAT YOU NEED TO GET WELL

Confessing you made the choice that traps you is not the real story. The real story is that God has already given you the power to be set free. God did not wait for you to discover you needed Him. He forgave you of all the messed up decisions and damaging choices you will ever make already. He is not limited to your understanding of what is wrong with you. God is already at work in you doing what you need to have done as you turn to Him in faith.

This truth is the final lesson you need to know. I learned it first from the author of Hebrews, who challenges his readers to "approach God's throne of grace with confidence, so that we may *receive mercy and find grace* to help us in our time of need." (Hebrews 4:16) And when you are choosing to get well *is* one of your greatest times of need.

Mercy and grace are what you get from God for this journey. Each of these gives you something you desperately need.

Mercy is given by God to those who are part of His family. In the Bible, this is called a covenant, a deep, unbreakable relationship. In this relationship, God's love is the defining feature." Because He loves us, He is totally committed to changing us to become like Jesus. But we mess up even after we are included in this covenant.

God, who never breaks His promises because He cannot lie, offers us mercy when we turn back to Him from our mess. This is the security of the covenant. God will never throw you out, get tired of your failures or abandon you. He will not only be merciful to you because you belong to Him, He will pursue you when you wander away into a mess.

Believe me, you will need mercy every day. So does everyone who belongs to God's family. So make sure to ask for it as soon as you realize you need it.

Grace meets a different need. Grace is a gift of empowerment from God. What I mean is that God, who knows you are unable to fix yourself, has given you power in the person of the Spirit. The Spirit lives in you. As you face the temptation of sinning again or feel overwhelmed by sadness or shame, God's Spirit is there to do for you what you cannot do for yourself.

To give a human example of the difference, if a murderer is taken into the family of the person he killed, and adopted as a son—that is mercy. But mercy cannot make that man good or change his desires when another relationship goes sour and his anger pushes him to kill somebody else. It is the work of grace that empowers him to discard his murderous heart, to lose the desire for revenge, and to become a peace-filled person. Only by God actively working by His grace inside this man's heart does real transformation—becoming the son he was adopted to be—take place.

God gives you grace so you can be freed from the *sin in me* choices you have made. Sin addiction is much more powerful than you are. Grace will deliver you from its power. And grace also is given to heal you. *Hurt of the heart* stays inside you because you have no power to heal yourself. But God does, and this is why you need grace.

You also need grace because your damaged emotions (feelings) will lie to you at the drop of a hat. Your inner voice will tell you to do irrational things and believe stupid ideas. I have sat with more than one person who was convinced that killing himself would free his family from the burden he felt he was to them. This is damaged emotions talking stupid and trying to convince you to follow their advice. You will quit jobs with no future one in sight at their prompting. You may walk away from the best relationships you have because your emotions will outright lie to you.

The Spirit is your goof-proof guide. He will heal your damaged emotions *when you ask him to* so you won't fall prey to their lies. This kind of grace is what you need, because without the Spirit nothing would change. You might resist for a while, but in the end find yourself still being relentlessly drawn deeper into the craziness of the lies Satan is telling you through your damaged emotions.

Receiving mercy and obtaining grace from the Father whose love for you is unbreakable so you can be transformed is the good news of Jesus. He made the way for you to be reconciled to this Father when you were His enemy. Keep telling yourself this good news. It's not about what you deserve. It's about what you get.

Do not think that you are flawed for life. Someone who was trapped by this lie was Katie. She was a pretty middle-schooler, on the cheerleading squad with plenty of friends, enjoying a carefree teenage life. Until the day a boy gave her a picture of an extremely overweight person and said it looked like her. She froze inside and went from carefree to being in bondage to the lie that her body was flawed. All through high school she lived with eating disorders that caused her weight to swing wildly up and down as she tried to comfort her painful wound with disastrous *sin in me* choices. She hated herself, her body—her life. Then at 21, she was set free from her eating disorders and self-hatred by saying 'Yes' to Jesus' question. After many desperate attempts to find freedom on her own, she received the mercy and grace she needed to be transformed.[1]

WHAT ELSE YOU NEED TO KNOW

Notice one more thing about the guy at the Bethesda pool. We don't know his name. His only identity is being sick for 38 years. There are a lot of stories about people like this who met Jesus; The five-time-divorcee-and-living-with-someone woman by the well in John 4; Ten lepers looking for healing in Luke 17; A deranged man with legion of demons in him in Mark 5; The woman caught in adultery in John 8.

We only know them by their reputation. This was the identity they were known by when they met Jesus. They were stuck with it. You may feel just like them—that you have an identity and you're stuck with it. Stuck identities are limitless—alcoholic, liar, two-faced, rude, insensitive, panicky, gossip, loud-mouth, nerdy, negative, unkind, druggie, lecherous, withdrawn, shopaholic, shallow, sarcastic, stupid, controller—too many to mention. Or, like Katie, someone stuck you with it, but you have not been able to shake it off.

Jesus came not just to heal and deliver, but to restore your identity. You are not the identity that has trapped you. You are Zack, Ian, Sara, Evie, Kristen, John, Kevin, Piers, Atari, Joe, Peter, Charles, _____ (write in your name). You are going to be known as the person you were created to be. No matter who calls you by your stuck identity, even if it is your closest friend or even yourself, Jesus is going to remove it and call you by his name for you, a real name, the one that reflects your whole, healthy self.

You are already more than that stuck identity. You are God's child. Your identity is wrapped up in Jesus. I say this because God has already decided to transform you so you will share Jesus' character (Romans 8:29). God, who invites us to call Him 'Father,' has made you a co-heir with Jesus, giving you assets and rights you might not know you have. These truths, which are recorded right in the Bible, are God's counterbalance to Satan's lies about who you are:

- You are at peace with God—He is not against you in any way. Romans 5:1
- You are His masterpiece. (Ephesians 2:10)
- You are handpicked by God to be holy and blameless. (Ephesians 1:3-4)
- You are treasured. (1 Peter 2:9)
- You are irreplaceable. (1 Thessalonians 1:4)
- Nothing will ever separate you from God's love. (Romans 8:35-39)
- You are so loved that you were worth dying for. (1 John 3:16)
- You will never be condemned by the Father. (Romans 8:1)
- You do not need to worry that you will be lost again. (John 10:28-29)
- You get to live a new life. (Romans 6:4)
- You have been set free to live. (Galatians 5:1)
- You always have Jesus and the Father living inside you. (John 14:23)
- Your life will make a difference because he chose you. (John 15:16)

These truths may not seem real to you yet, but they will when you are set free from your anxiety and fears. I encourage you to take another step, which is to pursue intimacy with God. Why? Because you do not have the ability to change your mind about the lie that keeps you trapped or to heal your damaged emotions. For you to come to trust God's strength in this process, you are going to have to know Him better. This will make sense. Keep reading...

[1] Katie Farrell https://dashingdish.com/blog/dashing-devotional-have-you-believed-a-lie

7. HOW GOD FITS INTO THIS JOURNEY

HOW YOU GET WELL

REMEMBER THAT Romans 8:29 says God has already decided to shape your life along the same lines as the life of his Son? Meaning that you will become just, loving, wise in the way Jesus is shown in the Bible—treating hurting people with kindness and challenging the hurtful people to see themselves as they are, and change. This is what transformation is all about. God is changing you so that your true self will emerge. No matter how unhappy or messed up you think you are, no matter how anxious and fearful you feel, God is going to make you whole because He loves you.

So here is something you need to know to move forward. *Only God can fix you.* Other people can love you, can offer you wisdom and guidance away from destructive behavior. They can surround you with protection and challenge your false thinking. But no one you know or will ever meet can actually change you inside except God.

I know a lot of people who are not convinced this is true. I have a dear friend who has stayed trapped for years because she thought she could find another way to health. She tried counseling, getting a mentor, joining support groups, accountability to others who called and asked personal questions to see if she was okay, and volunteering to help others. None of these things were bad for her. It's just that she used these approaches to avoid dealing with the real question she would not face with God: Why do I feel unvalued? Nothing she did could heal her pain or free her from the *sin in me* choices she constantly made trying to comfort her sense of worthlessness.

To be transformed you need power. Power beyond anything you have in yourself. Getting well is not a self-renovation project. You cannot fix yourself because you did not make yourself. What you did do is mess yourself up, but you have no idea how to put the pieces back into place. What you have to accept is that only God can fix your mess. God thought you up and He alone knows what He created you to be. He alone has the power to restore what's broken inside to wholeness.

Satan is counting on you swallowing the lie that you can fix yourself—or that, if you fail, there is no hope for you. His lie tells you, "It's no use going on because you blew the chance you had." Truthfully, no matter how many times you have tried to fix yourself and failed, God is still open to you right now. He is waiting for you to be with Him so He can do in you what you can *never* do for yourself.

But understand that being transformed is not *your* goal. It's *God's* goal for you. So often people get more anxious by thinking they have to change themselves right now! I need to be perfect. I need to grow up. Get my head in the game. You think this way because parents, teachers or coaches have been hammering you with these ideas all your life.

This is not how God thinks about you. He knows the way in which you will be healed and freed. He is not anxious about the pace at which you comply. You don't have to beat yourself up if you don't change right away when you come to God. Instead, He asks you to trust Him, to enjoy your relationship with Him—to *rest*.

What I can tell you from experience is when God heals the *hurt of your heart*, your *sin in me* choice has nothing it can hook into. It no longer offers you anything that you need. Then you find that your symptoms just go away. This is what it means to be transformed by God. Your symptoms will disappear as you deepen your relationship with God.

A RELATIONSHIP WITH THE REAL GOD

You will get well as you develop an intimacy with the real God. This truth is at the heart of all I know and teach. Not religious enthusiasm. Not religious activities. This is not about going to church more often or volunteering to serve in some mission. Intimacy is knowing God in the same way you know your closest friend. It is about how you focus your mind on Him, how you spend your time with Him, how you talk to and hear from Him, how you use what He has already given you.

The most important step before you is getting to know God better. You see, the Father is real. He is not real when you decide He is real. He just is. But up to now, you may not know Him very well, so He seems to you like one of those storybook characters—Santa Claus, the Tooth Fairy or Prince Charming—that your folks told you about when you were younger.

I think a lot of people share this outlook on God because He cannot be seen by their eyes. This is exactly why Jesus came. He told his followers when they saw him, they were also seeing the Father. God put on flesh years ago and lived among people. He knew that people needed to connect with Him so that they would not only trust Him, but also so He could defeat the very thing they feared the most. To paraphrase the writer of Hebrews 2:14-15, God came among us as a human so, in Jesus, He could break Satan's death grip over humanity and free us from slavery to our fear of death.

Your unfinished business—the anxiety and fear you live with—is rooted in why Jesus came to die on the cross. His resurrection from death is a demonstration of God's power that is able to set you free. This is why there is hope for you no matter how messed up you may feel. God, who lives in you, is greater than Satan, who lies to keep you trapped and afraid. God has already taken away Satan's control over you. This is the real God using His power for you before you ever gave Him a thought.

What I am going to teach you are three practices that I found to help people to focus on knowing God intimately so they can trust Him when He tells you to pick up your mat and walk. I call them the 'done' disciplines. They are disciplines because you have to practice them. That's because they are not what you might normally think about doing when it comes to your relationship with God. But they will make sense as you do them regularly. Also, they are 'done' disciplines because they focus you on understanding and making use of what God has already done for you in Jesus.

REST

Think about a day when you were free from every demanding responsibility that the people in your world had put on you. What did you do that day? Did you spend time with someone special? Did you get away to be alone? Did you get to do the things you like? Whatever your answer, this is called rest—getting to abandon structured activities to do the things closest to your heart.

The first 'done' discipline is actually getting to rest. Many people think that the main characteristic of being a believer is work, work and more work. We think God wants us to be busy for Him. But since Jesus shows us what the Father is like, one significant incident in his life gives us the real picture. It was when he was visiting the home of Mary and Martha. Martha was franticly running around trying to get everything ready. Mary was over there with Jesus and the other guests just hanging out with him. When Martha complained that she needed Mary's help, Jesus quietly pointed out that, though he appreciated Martha's activities on his behalf, Mary had made a better choice.

This is how it is for God and you. He appreciates whatever you do for Him, but what you need is to be with Him. You can exhaust yourself doing what you think God demands of you and miss the rest He created you for.

I call rest 'being with God without an agenda.' Coming to God without a list of things to pray about or a bunch of Bible verses you have to read; resting from all your efforts to be good for God; resting from all the requirements someone has made you think will make you a better person and just being yourself with God (who never is embarrassed about you or angry with you). Rest means you let God get a word in edgewise about who you really are instead of you trying to explain yourself to Him.

Rest is like just being with someone you like and letting the time unfold. It means being ready to listen and hear what God has for you—mercy, grace, love, restoration. Talking about whatever you are thinking about. Listening to the reply and learning step by step to let down your guard; to say nothing, but drink in the closeness of the Father; to sing to Him; to be unafraid. This is how you build an intimate relationship with God.

I already know why you will find this hard when you start practicing rest, because it was hard for me. Like everyone else in our videoed, internet connected, visually stimulated world, you have a very busy mind. It is hard to focus on one thing for more than a couple of minutes at a time, much less give your full attention to knowing God better.

So let me offer you a simple first step. Look up Hebrews 4:16 in God's company and think about it together. Recognize that you are coming into your Father's presence and that you are there to receive mercy and grace—the features of His great love for you. Allow the Spirit to empower you to listen for His words of acceptance and affirmation for you. Do this every day as you start the morning, even if it is only for sixty seconds. You can call him God, Father, Jesus, Abba (Daddy)…whatever you want. Do not ask for anything, just receive what he wants to give. Rest in His power to remake your life and renew your mind. In time, you will come to rest with God longer and longer.

Below are some of the changes that I have experienced in my thinking because I learned to rest.

- On my own, I don't have the strength to beat what defeats me, but I am safe within God.
- I don't have the personal resources to fix myself, but God already knows this and accepts me.
- I don't have to clean up to be in God's presence. He never rejects me.
- I don't need to hide anything, since God already knows everything.
- I don't need to explain things to God. I just need to receive whatever God is giving me.

You will not grow in your ability to rest by a quick session or two with God. Knowing God better will mean you have to *make* time intentionally. You will never *find* time for this! You will have to get away from distractions. So choose a place where you are physically comfortable while you are with God. Make being alone with God a regular part of your life.

APPROPRIATE

Here is something else you need to practice in order to deepen your trust in God. This is the second 'done' discipline—to appropriate what God has already given you. If you are unfamiliar with the word 'appropriate,' think of it in this way...

In my home we have a refrigerator in which everything is fair game. The other day I stowed in there a nice piece of leftover steak in a to-go carton when I returned from a long day on the road. And then I told my wife I knew it would be eaten by our still-living-at-home son. Sure enough, the container was empty in the morning. My son, who of course knows that in our house all food is up for grabs in the refrigerator, claimed it as a midnight snack. This is appropriation—

freely taking what is there for you without hesitation. No begging. No fear. Your need filled at the moment you reach out to take. I cannot tell you how much this powerful discipline has freed me from one addictive sin after another over time.

God has filled up the refrigerator inside you with all that you need to live a whole and holy life. I used to wonder what this meant until one of my mentors explained to me what Paul was praying about in Ephesians 1:18-19. I paraphrase it here: "I pray that light would flood your mind so you would understand the hope to which God has called you, the riches of his glorious inheritance inside you and how He is working with incomparably great power in you who believe."

Let me unpack this for you. Do you ever feel lost, worthless, or useless? Do you ever feel empty and abandoned? Do you ever feel unable to obey what God has shown you to do? Here is why the done discipline of appropriation is so important for you in order to develop trust in God.

First let's talk about the word 'hope.' In the Bible, the word means something a little different from the way we use that word now. Hope in the Bible means you are expecting a sure thing—something that is really going to happen. It is both about being safe with God and being assured that He is working to make you whole—healing your pain and freeing you to be who you were created to be. When Satan lies to make you doubt that God has saved you or suggests that you are a mess that can never be redeemed, God has already given you a different future to look forward to that refutes those lies. All you have to do is take it because God has already given it to you.

The 'riches' tell you that whatever Jesus possesses is now yours, too. If you will read through Colossians and Ephesians, you will constantly see Paul saying you are 'in Jesus.' Being 'in Jesus' is a way of saying that your family tree has changed. You were born into Adam's family. As his descendent, you lost spiritual wisdom and power when Adam and Eve rejected God's reign over them. But now you belong to God's family in Jesus and everything he is or has is yours. Here is a taste of what you have from Ephesians 1:3-14:

- You are blessed with every spiritual blessing in Christ Jesus.
- God chose you in Christ Jesus.
- You are adopted in Christ Jesus, because this gives God great pleasure.
- God has freely given you His empowering presence in Christ Jesus in order to change you.
- God paid the price to get you out of the mess you were in by being in Christ Jesus.
- You are forgiven in Christ Jesus.
- God unsparingly used His power to change you, heaping riches of wisdom and understanding on you.
- God has already decided to put you into a situation where God is going to get His way.
- God has already decided that your life will be a display of His personal glory.
- Your salvation is already guaranteed by the Spirit.
- You are God's possession.

The power is about the Spirit's work in your life to do for you what you are not able to do for yourself. You cannot be obedient in your own strength or reform yourself to look and act like Jesus. Instead God does this in you by the Spirit as you, by faith, walk in humble obedience, knowing it is the Spirit's power accomplishing it in you.

Why should the 'done' discipline of appropriation be important for you? Like the rest of us, you will fail to get over your anxieties and fear using your own resources. Face it. *You* have nothing that works. But because of the good news of Jesus Christ, destruction and defeat will not be your future. Take what's yours already. Move forward in wholeness with God, empowered by the resources you have been given. As you do, you will see God's truth and power at work fixing your mess. And from then on you will trust Him even more.

I remember the time when I started my intentional pursuit of intimacy with God. The first thing He showed me was that I was to stop criticizing my wife. I was stunned. For one thing, I never had seen it as a problem. And also, I had been a criticizer all my life. I did not know how to just stop. So I told God that I could not do this in my own strength. I told him I knew that trying to change would only last a few weeks or days at the most. But I was willing to do it if the Spirit's power did it for me.

One year after this conversation with God, my wife wrote in her journal that the top reason she loved me was because I did not criticize her! God had changed me from a criticizer to a supporter of my wife. That would have not happened if I had not used the Spirit's power God had already put inside my inner refrigerator.

MEDITATE ON JESUS LOVE

No one wants to get close to a God they think is angry or disgusted with them. Unfortunately, many believers have been told this is exactly what God thinks of them when they fail to be good. But this is untrue. This typecasting of God makes Him out to be like a messed up human instead of the God who loved the world so much He sent His Son to die for it. He loves you and knew before He included you in His family that not only were you a mess, you would have a hard time all your life at being good. What the Bible says is that God does not condemn those who belong to Him (Romans 8:1).

I used to be afraid of God. I thought He was super disappointed with my behavior. I thought He would punish me for being such a mess. I discovered a lot of other people think the same thing. I remember while in my teens spending hours groveling before God because I felt His judgment, but not His love. So how did I ever come to trust Him with my life?

It started when I found out that I had created a made-up God in my mind. I had plastered the face of every unbending, stern authority figure I had met over the face of God—my unreasonable school principal, the grim-faced army officer that lived down the street, my humorless teachers, my parents. Each of them made me think that God was like them. Then one day, out of desperation, I met with God on different terms. I decided to take the Bible's word for it that God is love. I had just messed up again, but this time, instead of coming to God defensive and afraid, I would meet with Him as the loved child that I really was.

What I discovered that day was that nothing I did ever caused God to give up on me. I found Him laughing at my fears and learned He was ready to make me whole. That is the day I really fell in love with God. Our relationship has never been the same since.

To be able to draw close to God in intimacy, you will need to practice the third 'done' discipline of meditating on Jesus' love. You have to understand His love as deeply as you can because it is the most critical factor in overcoming your unfinished business. Knowing that you are in the personal grip of His love is your greatest security in this sometimes alarming process of transformation. It reminds you that you are safe with God.

Years ago Gerald May wrote a powerful book on grace in which he gave a picture of the faithfulness of God's love. He wrote:

God's love is more constant than human love can be. Human loving has its pure moments and parental love especially can sometimes express a likeness of God in its deep steadiness. But however solid it may be, human love is always prey to selfishness and distractions...It is not so with God's love. God goes on loving us regardless of who we are or what we do. This does not mean God is like a permissive human parent who makes excuses and ignores the consequences of a child's behavior. In God's constantly respectful love, consequences of our actions are very real, and they can be horrible, and we are responsible. We are even responsible for the compulsive behaviors of our addictions. The freedom God preserves in us has a double edge. On the one hand, it means God's love and empowerment are always with us. On the other, it means there is no authentic escape from the truth of our choices. But even when our choices are destructive and their consequences are hurtful, God's love remains unwavering. [1]

To be safe on your true journey of being conformed to Jesus' image, knowing this unwavering love matters for you. In Ephesians 3:17-19, Paul prays that his readers, who already are loved deeply, would have the power to grasp this love of Christ. Understanding it is the necessary ingredient for being filled up with God's presence inside you. Grasping this love has been made possible because you have the mind of Christ. His love is what brings you to trust the safeness of God in the middle of your mess when you are full of anxiety and fear. It gives you hope that you will see the end of your unfinished business when no end seems in sight.

In fact, grasping Jesus' love does more than make you feel safe. The reason someone becomes addicted to *sin in me* to start with is because they were looking for love in the wrong place. You were created for love—to be loved and give love. But *hurt in the heart* damages your ability to receive love. You even push it away because your damaged emotions tell you that you cannot believe anyone really loves you. That is what the hurt is in you. Your heart is love-starved wherever you are wounded. When you finally begin to understand Jesus' love, you will find that:

Jesus' love restores your ability to receive love properly.

Jesus' love is the love you need to be healed

Jesus' love is bottomless and will make you able to live at peace with yourself and others

God will never stop loving you no matter how messed up you are.

Knowing Jesus' love is the true path to being free from anxiety and fear.

So how do you mediate on Jesus' love? You have to again make time to do this. I do this regularly. Asking the Spirit to guide me, I think about how God has loved me when I feel unlovable. I ponder how much God has shown His love for me through His forgiveness and acceptance of me. I ask Jesus to give me insight into why he loves me. How deep is it? How wide is it? How high and long does it stretch? This meditation offers a daily reminder to me of who I am to Him. I actually say out loud while I am in His presence, "I know you love me. I am safe." I hear Him affirm this in my heart, even on days when my wounded emotions are raw and I feel the beckoning of the sin in me—especially on those days.

This time I spend focused on Jesus' love has convinced me of this incredible love of Jesus, who came to show us what God is like. God is no longer a specter of fear for me. It can be this way for you as well. Take the time to practice this third 'done' discipline so that you will know and not doubt that Jesus' love is not like the many other loves that have failed you. Know this love will never dry up on you.

INTIMACY WITH GOD ANSWERS THE QUESTION WHY

You might wonder, "Why did God let bad stuff happen to me if He is so loving?" A question like this cannot be fully answered this side of the grave. But I can tell you that pursuing intimacy with God will deepen your trust in Him. And it takes a deeper trust in God to allow Him to heal and deliver. However, if you choose to invest in the relationship God offers, you will find your unanswered questions are not as important as the way God uses all the events of your life, including the bad and ugly ones you struggle with, to bring about wholeness in you.

Joni Eareckson Tada was just seventeen when she misjudged the shallowness of the water and dove into the Chesapeake Bay. She broke her neck and became a quadriplegic, paralyzed from the shoulders down. Suffering depression through her long rehab, she drew a self-portrait holding charcoal pencils between her teeth. She wrote that this sketch said it all:

Oh God, this is now my life! You actually expect me to do this?

I was once the 17-year-old who retched at the thought of living life without a working body. I hated my paralysis so much I would drive my power wheelchair into walls, repeatedly banging them until they cracked. Early on, I found dark companions who helped me numb my depression with scotch-and-cola. I just wanted to disappear. I wanted to die.

During this time, my Bible study friend Steve Estes shared ten little words that set the course for my life: "God permits what he hates to accomplish what he loves." Steve explained it this way: "Joni, God allows all sorts of things he doesn't approve of. God hated the torture, injustice, and treason that led to the crucifixion. Yet he permitted it so that the world's worst murder could become the world's only salvation. In the same way, God hates spinal cord injury, yet he permitted it for the sake of Christ in you—as well as in others."

Somehow, I did it. Or, the Holy Spirit did it in me. As of today, I've done it for 50 years. I really would rather be in this wheelchair knowing Jesus as I do than be on my feet without him.[1]

I have no way of knowing how you have been damaged. You probably never broke your neck, but you may have been bullied,

117

ridiculed, neglected, sexually used or personally traumatized by a physical disability. You may feel that no one loves you, least of all God. But this also is not true. But God knows you by name. The Bible says God engraved you on the palms of His hands (Isaiah 49:16).

You will know this for yourself when you begin to pursue intimacy with Him. You will only find satisfactory answers to your questions from Him alone. Your trust in Him will build because you will begin to know God in a personal way. You will spend time hanging out with Him, letting Him whisper love to you, learning His path for you. It will lead to confidence in your relationship with Him.

It is this kind of trust that intimacy with God produces. You will find you can say anything—you can confess sin, can admit temptations are attractive, ask hard questions, wish for a different life, be honest about being angry with Him,—without fearing that He will break up with you. You find you are finally safe to be yourself before Him, because He welcomes such honesty. He is like no earthly parent you ever had. He is the supreme Father who knew you could not become all you were created to be without His power. He knows your unfinished business better than you do, still there is no condemnation in Him. He is able to free you from your anxiety and fears.

Intimacy with God will also give you hope that you will be healed and freed from your anxiety and fear. Real transformation requires a Person to empower it in you. So instead of the feeling that God is looking judgmentally over your shoulder, you find God is lovingly participating in the journey with you. Through intimacy you discover God's unwavering acceptance of the responsibility to transform you into what you were created to be. Knowing Him deeply will give you a place of refuge when *sin in me* applies pressure to your damaged emotions with a cheap substitute for healing.

[1]https://www.thegospelcoalition.org/article/reflections-on-50th-anniversary-of-my-diving-accident

8. YOU CAN'T DO THIS ALONE

YOU ARE NOT MEANT TO TRAVEL TOWARD HEALTH ALONE

SHE RAN SCREAMING out of the room where we were meeting. Her background in the occult—tarot cards and psychic readings—clashed with her sense of God's presence and she ran. After she ran another young woman dodged through the parking lot to discover what frightened her and to let her know she was safe.

She reluctantly allowed herself to be talked into staying. She came back the next week however. Likeable, outgoing and funny, she was included in the life of the community without pressure being put on her to explain what was going on inside her. The group, to make sure she felt safe, made some small, but important, changes in their gatherings so she would not be triggered by fear.

Then she brought a friend of hers who she thought would benefit from being around the people who make up this spiritual community.

And then she brought another. Slowly, she realized she was safe. She confided her secrets to someone who helped her trust God with them. She discovered she was not alone on her journey to wholeness—and God changed her life.

What do I mean by 'community'? Included in this word is the idea of being a real family, where people want to help each other get better…a place where people keep each other's backs…a group where people do not let someone just disappear, but go, find and bring back those who seeming to drop out. Where people are honest, kind, and hold each other up. More importantly, a community is a place where people help us to know God better, pray for us and love us with the love God gave them. Community is the group of people who like us as we are, but want us see us grow healthy.

Perhaps you feel alone. You feel you have no one you can trust with your haunting secrets. Perhaps you have been betrayed when you tried to share something before and got into trouble. Or judged by people you thought would understand. So you have bottled up your anxiety and fears and stuffed them all inside so you can protect yourself.

This is not a good thing. You were not made to be alone. Jesus understood this. He came to build his church into a place where people will not only proclaim good news, but where those who belong will take care of each other. As you flip through the Bible, you see directives for believers to, "love each other," "bear each other's burdens," "encourage each other," "serve each other," "forgive each other," and "be kind and compassionate to each other," along with forty-six other ways to be real family to each other.

You need a community, a real family, to help you on this journey to wholeness. One reason is that your journey is lifelong. Imagine living your whole life alone with no one who understands or is concerned for you. It would be like living your life out in the manner of Ebenezer Scrooge from *A Christmas Carol*. Now there was a guy with unfinished business. Lost his mother as a boy, hated by his father, abandoned to make his own way before he was out of his teens, he grew old being a cutthroat businessman who was miserly and friendless. Sure, there were people in his life—Jacob Marley, Bob Cratchit, his nephew Fred, his housekeeper. But by his own choice he had no community. He didn't want one, so he chose to be alone.

What will you become if all your life you choose to have no one? No one to trust with your deepest hurts? No one who will be there to tell you truths you need to hear?

A second reason you need community is, since of the Fall of Adam and Eve, humans have made this world into a tough place to live. It is not going to become safe and peaceful until what the Bible calls the Day of the Lord—God's Day, when God puts everything back together as it was meant to be. But right now God is at work through Jesus healing and making people healthy.

Your life is tough and your family and friends' lives are, as well. Some people you will meet have experienced tougher lives than you. This is why you need to band together and help each other for the duration. It is a faith journey with God and others, making sense out of the fire swamp that this world is—and at the same time, encouraging each other on to healing and deliverance from your unfinished business.

But what kind of community? All of you belong to a family community, for better or worse. You have a group of friends. Maybe a school or work community. But the kind of community you need most is a safe spiritual community. That community hopefully will include people from your other communities. However personal healing only happens in communities where those who belong are safe people to be around.

Unsafe spiritual communities may seem like they are about becoming more like Jesus, but under the surface they encourage people do sad and stupid things. One was led by a guy who really wanted to help teens have better lives. But when one teenager in the group got frustrated with her parents, instead of helping her work with her mom and dad to bring about healing and change, he helped her plan to run away. It did not end well. This taught me that just because someone cares about you does not mean they are safe.

A safe spiritual community is one where people want you to get healthy; where people know that only God can heal you; where people are grounded in eternal truth; where people are patient with you until you feel it is the right moment to reveal your inner anxieties and fears. It's a place where no one is thrown under the bus when they mess up: where no one suggests action plans that only make life worse: where no one tries to regulate your every thought and action; where no one posts the secrets you share to others who do not need to know.

A safe spiritual community is one where people get honest about themselves. One safe spiritual community I was part of started to help a friend who was blowing up his life. The other three guys wanted to walk him back to health. Except that, when we began to meet weekly, the rest of us got honest. We had unfinished business too. We realized we were not just there to help our friend. We were there to encourage each other on our own journey. So we had no reason to judge each other. We recognized ourselves in each others' messy stories. We told each other the truth, pointed to Jesus as the one who made us whole and, in time, became more of the person we were meant by God to be. The friend we wanted to help got his life back together as well.

A safe spiritual community is one where people—even people who seem very different from you—become family. Here's why you need to find a safe spiritual community. In that kind of community you will be loved with Spirit-empowered love. I found that in each of my safe communities the friendships kept developing until we became a real family. Like Sam, for instance. When he first joined our community he wasn't sure he even liked me because he had some serious unfinished business. His background was so different from mine. But I loved him when he was really messed up. Now, years later, he calls me or I call him regularly because we are as close as brothers. Our relationship got that way because God changed us inside, broke down our defenses and bonded us together in love. You need this as much as I do.

A safe spiritual community is a place where you can share your secrets safely. Not the first day probably, nor the second week. But we are all looking for a place where we can be encouraged to get freedom from what we are feeling inside.

In the Bible, James teaches believers to "confess your sins to each other and pray for each other so that you may be healed. The prayer of a righteous person is powerful and effective." (James 5:16). What James is saying is that secret-keeping is not the pathway to healing. Confession is. No longer hiding your sin, your damaging thoughts, the lies you believe or your pain. No longer defending your destructive behavior as normal, but getting prayed for instead.

Someone I know well was asked by a young man how he could find the same kind of freedom he saw in my friend. My friend sat him down, looked him in the eye and said, "Tell me three sins you have never told to anyone else." The shocked man looked at him for a long minute and then blurted out three long-standing issues he had been ashamed to tell anyone before. My friend's response was, "Praise God! Do you want something to drink?" Again the young man was startled and asked how the request for a drink fit into the conversation.

My friend told him that he himself was thirsty and, "By the way, isn't it great that you can confess your sin without someone jumping down your throat in judgment?" Then my friend prayed for him and he was really healed. This newly freed man went forward in his life telling others about his confession, how it released him from addictive sin and how they also could be set free by confessing their sins. This is what confessing sin in community will do for you as well.

What I love best about safe spiritual communities is that they do it Jesus' way. There is no condemnation. No shaming a person to try to make them behave. Being committed to doing whatever it takes to mend broken relationships when people get upset with each other—or helping someone who has messed up get healthy again. I find hope in these kinds of communities, because they remind me that God is real and that the good news of Jesus is true.

FINDING COMMUNITY

So how do you find this kind of community? They're not as uncommon as you think. But you have to look for them, even in your own church. Sometimes you have to ask people to form one with you to get this kind of community. Not all groups are healthy even in a church. But do keep looking, because there is a safe person out there who is ready to help you. One day, when my life was coming apart, I went looking for Tom.

I had known Tom for some years, but had never talked deeply with him. Yet I felt drawn to him in my crisis. Could I tell him my secrets? Would he listen and not judge me harshly? What would happen if Tom told someone else what I shared with him? You notice I was concerned about his reaction to me. I knew I was taking a risk to trust Tom.

But what I found was by listening to what the Spirit was saying through Tom, I was moved from brokenness to wholeness. He probed my relationship to my parents. He told me that I was thinking wrong about why I was messed up. He said it was my choices rather than the actions of a friend that kept me trapped. He reminded me that God's Spirit was in me to give me power to change. He guided me to pursue healing instead of hoarding my hurts. Everything he said was gentle, but direct. That is what being in a safe spiritual community is all about.

Here are the four signs I look for in finding a safe spiritual community today:

First: I look for the right characteristics in the people who make up the community. The day I knew I had to deal with my unfinished business, I went looking for Tom because I knew that I needed him. I knew Tom was a safe person because other people besides me went looking for him for the same reason.

What made Tom safe? I think first of all, he was unshockable. He knew people had a dark side and went to dark places in their lives. He had heard many stories from people who needed a rock to cling to instead of having rocks thrown at them. Nothing upset him or surprised him. And no one who spent time with him was abused.

What Tom displayed was the fruit of the Spirit. Paul talks about the fruit of the Spirit in Galatians 5:22-23. This fruit consists of love, joy, peace, patience, kindness, goodness gentleness, faithfulness and self-control. All of them matter, but the two that mean the most to me when it comes to finding a safe spiritual community are kindness and gentleness. I look for kindness because I do not want people beating me up. I am already doing that to myself. I need someone who will step in and stop the pounding, who will tell me that God loves me, that there is hope and healing. I need somebody who will not allow me to run away, but draw me in. Someone who will treat me like they want to be treated themselves. That's kindness.

Gentleness is different. The word itself comes from the idea of training horses. As big and powerful as these animals are, they can be gentled to allow a little child to guide them with nothing but a bridle. Gentle means power (horse) under control (bridle).

Why I look for gentleness is that gentleness breeds gentleness. Safe spiritual communities are full of people who are out of control and needing help. A gentle person will be firm and direct with them, but not angry and mean. Gentleness does not mean being too weak to confront or easily cowed by someone's crazy behavior. Instead, it is the strength to hang in there with the person—or being available to those who want to run away—until the person is ready to get well.

Tom listened to my rambling stories. Then gently, he told me that what I thought was the problem was not the problem. He asked deep questions. He made me explore reality. I found the time with Tom was emotionally exhausting, but he never made me sorry I was with him. Tom told me truth that I needed to hear and God used it to transform me bigtime.

Some people who try to help are not safe because they are not kind or gentle. What they tell you may be important, but they use it as an accusation rather than a truth to set you free. There is harshness in their tone, as if it is their goal to cut your heart out with their words. Harshness is telling someone to "put on your big boy pants," instead of inviting him on a journey to maturity. Harshness is fat-shaming a young woman instead of showing her how the life she really wants is being sabotaged by her eating habits.

I have seen the voice of kindness and gentleness many times in safe communities. One woman gently pointing out to an oblivious young woman what her proud heart was doing to those close to her. In her brokenness, she was tromping all over the emotions of her family, creating impenetrable walls between her and them. A person boldly told another that his anger problem was not about his friend, but was there because he had never forgiven his father. Because these truths were kindly and gently given, they had a great impact on the people to whom they were said.

Second: I test the waters. Do these people have a record of being safe? I sought out Tom because of what others told me about him. I knew he was safe before I spent any time with him myself.

I have been part of a number of safe spiritual communities—am in one now. It matters to me that people are safe with us. So here are some things to watch for as you seek out your community.

1. They talk *with* people instead of *about* people. They do not talk negatively when someone's name comes up, whether that person is inside or outside the community.

2. They are not put off by bad behavior because they understand that it only reflects what is going on in a person's heart. They encourage people to talk through disagreements, to let go of unhealthy habits that are hurting them like gossip, overeating, or hating, and remind them that God loves them and can heal whatever they are trying to drown out with these habits. They are not put off by bad behavior because they understand that it only reflects what is going on in a person's heart.

3. They *include* rather than *exclude* people. Everyone is welcomed and pursued if they drift away. And it is not hard for someone new to break into the group. In other words, I am looking to see if they know how to be family with me.

4. They make friends with broken people rather than push them away. They know they can be used by God to help them. They expect these broken people to get well in time, instead of continuing to struggle with their unfinished business.

Third: I ask God to show me if this is the right community for me. I don't always know what is going on under the surface in a community. But God does. I trust he will show me. And I look to see if the community is centered on God's truth. This is where the rubber meets the road. There are a lot of 'truths' out there. But I have learned not to trust everyone's version of the truth because too often people end up being misguided.

So I am looking for how they understand God's authority. How seriously they take the Bible. Whether they use it to prop up their personal truths or let it challenge and change their lives. I have to know that to them, the Word of God is sharper than a double-bladed sword than can pierce down into the essential person and reveal to them the truth of what they think and how they decide to live their lives.

Fourth: I invest time weekly. There is no such thing as instant community. It will take you a huge investment of time and honesty to develop this kind of community. You have to be there with others when they need you and not just show up when you are needy. When you are together you aren't distracted by cell phones and you don't just hang out all the time--you really listen, you ask hard questions, you sit with people when they are hurting, you laugh along with them. You have to make time to be with others in your community a priority. To be available for the when-you-need-me moments. If you truly want real community instead of just a social group, you will have to go through uncomfortable times of getting to know each other, annoying each other, and making mistakes until you come trust each other with the worst as well as the best in you. Trust comes with walking through fire, rain, blood and mud together.

The hardest part will be giving up your scary secrets. You desperately need a safe spiritual community where you can tell what you have hidden in your heart. I can count on only one hand people I know who have healed *without* sharing their most painful secrets. I myself would have never made it without that kind of community around me. I had to share my secrets so they would lose power over me.

Do not give up on seeking out a community like this. God is already preparing it—preparing the people you need—for you. And for others you will bring to it as you heal. Look for these signs and be part of the best family you will ever know who will join with you in pursuing God-given freedom and spiritual, emotional and mental health.

9. RESTART YOUR JOURNEY

DONT HANG BACK...RESTART AND GET MOVING!

THERE ARE SOME moments I will always remember. Like when Jackson passionately responded 'Yes' to the question, "Do you want to get well?" He had been living with lies so long that they were his life. He had been stuck waiting for God to somehow free him. The next time I saw him, he came up to me to let me know he was moving forward in freedom. The relaxed joy on his face was in total contrast from our first meeting. His faith community is giving him all the support he needs because it is full of people who are also on a journey with God.

Getting to guide people to freedom from their anxieties and fears is what gets me up every morning. So it bugs me when people choose to wait around instead of allowing God to restart their lives. They might be extremely interested in what I teach. They really enjoy learning the basic principles. "Eye-opening!" some say. But they are not *going* anywhere. A year later I may see them again only to find them still running in place, maybe with a better understanding of why they are stuck, but refusing to make the decision to get well.

This is opposite to the world of Jesus. He said to the man by the pool of Bethesda, "Take up your bed and walk,"—and down the road the man went. In Jesus' Kingdom, people are healed in real time, souls are knit back together, and sin loses its addictive power. People get to walk—to leap, frolic, skip, hop, spring, run, and experience forward motion in their spiritual, emotional, and mental lives (by every movement word in the thesaurus). In other words, standing still is also your choice, but it does not have to be your destiny—or your destination.

PICK UP YOUR MAT

So, *do you want to get well*? I have asked Jesus' question to a lot of people over the years. Nick was one who said 'No.' He thought he could duck the issues of his life and avoid the destruction they were about to deliver to his door. He even formed his own posse to protect him from having to face getting well. I tried to warn him nothing he could do would keep the destruction at bay.

I am glad that many more have said 'Yes.' Their lives stand as a beacon to others of how freeing Jesus' offer is. Like Austin. As talented as he was, he was always living in the pit of despair that he would ever amount to anything. His unfinished business included growing up in an explosive household full of pettiness and denial, covered over with religious activity. Then Jesus invited him to get well and he did. Today his whole neighborhood is being changed by his gentle and kind ways of loving messed up people.

Jesus invites you to trust him, pick up your mat, and walk. This invitation from Jesus answers a question I often get asked. The person asking usually is hearing transformational ideas for the first time. And so he or she might ask some form of the following: "If God is the one who does the changing in me, am I supposed to just do nothing at all, just sit like a pawn on a chessboard and wait for Him to move me somehow?" To answer this, I have to be clear on an important distinction. There is a difference between *magic* and *faith*.

Sometimes religious people confuse miracles with magic. ~~The idea of using~~ magic is about having power over an object or person. The object or person has no say in whether they can be manipulated. In magic, objects and persons are merely passive and are changed or used whether or not they want to be. This is not true of miracles. Miracles require a faith response from the people involved. Miracles are joint ventures between God and people.

People who approach God as if He is a divine magician look for Him to abracadabra them into wholeness while they watch. The trick Jesus pulled at the Bethesda pool—"That was pure magic."—is their way of seeing it. "God does it all while we do nothing," is not really what this story tells us. It never is about a man passively being magically healed. Yes, Jesus did display his divine power, and it is unequalled by any trick performed by any magician. But the suspenseful part of the story is whether or not the man would actually pick up his mat.

Engaging in the transformational process is a lot like physical exercise. Picture a room full of somewhat overweight, out-of-shape people listening to a talk on the importance of exercising. Then they watch some YouTube videos on how to exercise. Would you really be surprised if all these people in the room were still unfit a year later? Physical fitness does not happen when someone understands the theory of working out. People become fit through engaging in consistent, regular exercise. And people become transformed when by faith they act on what Jesus offers them.

Jesus is not offering us a magical solution for the symptoms you have. He is offering you restoration and health. But you have to pick up your mat. You have to say 'Yes' to the offer. You have to, by faith, respond to the command to get up, rather than thinking it *may* be true, that you would *love to see it* be true, and *someday it may* come true. Passively waiting for God to do more while you watch is the same as saying 'No.' Faith says, "Okay, if you tell me to do this, I will trust that you will actually keep me on my feet and give me the strength to walk home with this mat in my hands."—and then seeing God do just that.

Responding in faith to the question, "Do you want to get well?" does not mean you will automatically 'feel' safe. Your damaged emotions may still fight you for control over your life. Damaged emotions are dedicated to the hopeless quest of finding a safe place in the world away from your pain. You may still want to agree with your damaged emotions that making a *sin in me* choice is your best option. Your damaged emotions are familiar, they seem to tell you truth—but they can't be trusted! They have already led you into dark places, why would you trust them now? You have to ask God to empower you to know this is true and firmly remind yourself of it every time your emotions scream for you to stick to the destructive course.

Picking up your mat means you trust God's offer for real healing. That act of faith can be upsetting, uncomfortable, inconvenient. But you will have to choose it to get to where you really want to go. And then you will have to continue to trust God, since faith walking is always harder than it looks from the sidelines—because you, like everyone else, are more damaged than you realize.

One of the people I watched who learned to trust God over her emotions was a young woman coming off drugs. One week she'd come out with, "I don't know if I will make it through this next week! Things are such a mess." The next week it would be, "None of my friends are calling and checking to see if I'm okay." Zoe always started our meetings with something new that was going wrong. It was like she needed things to be bad. Zoe was just learning how to trust God. But as she healed she kept clinging to new reasons why everything was falling apart: a car problem, her boss's expectations, her friends. After weeks of this continual parade of personal disasters, I finally asked "Zoe, do you only feel normal when you are in a crisis?"

That made her think. She began to realize how much she was letting her emotions continue to speak for her. Slowly, she allowed God to heal and rein them back into their proper boundaries. She has gone on into adulthood and to a fruitful life with a husband who loves her deeply.

So what should you do? The first thing is to ask God to show you what He wants you to do. What form does His invitation to pick up your mat take? Does He want you to stop swearing? Do acts of kindness for people that you do not like? Be generous even when you face bills of your own? Stop complaining? Apologize to someone you wounded? Be at peace over a personal flaw or disability you cannot change? Give up an addictive behavior you still get pleasure out of? Confess something you're ashamed of? Forgive the offender? Don't *guess* at what your mat is—*ask God* and He will show you what you need to pick up that will make you healthy again.

And when you pick up your mat, you will find that Jesus has already given you the power to actually do whatever God has shown you. You will not have to rely on your own strength to get it done. But with your willingness to pick up that mat you will find the Spirit's strength, which we call *grace*.

You also will need to ask God to help you distinguish His voice from the voices of your damaged emotions so that you know this is the right mat to pick up. I discovered on my own journey the necessity of asking God to help me distinguish His voice because I was to ready to substitute my voice for His when it came to asking where my symptoms were coming from. I was wrong every time I depended on my own best thoughts. I stayed by the pool much longer than I had to when *my* voice overrode some truth I needed to get well.

How will you know you are hearing God's voice? Here are four guidelines that helped me:

First, I know I am hearing God because what I hear is an insight about myself, often a totally new thought that I never had before. When I stop doing all the talking and listen is when I hear these new thoughts from God.

Second, I know it is God speaking when I emotionally resonate with this new truth. It does not merely sound convincing or convicting. The new truth touches me in the deepest part of my soul when I hear it.

Third, When I hear this insight, I experience a sense of hope instead of despair. This is how I know it is from God and not Satan.

The enemy knows truth about me too. However, when Satan points out the truth about me, I feel defeated and exposed. When God speaks, He speaks as a Daddy who loves His child and wants me to be whole. Insight God gives causes me to be secure that I will come out in the end picking up my mat and walking.

Fourth, I know that I have heard an insight from God because it amazingly always gives me the desire to forgive. And I mean both forgiving the one who caused the *hurt of my heart* as well as accepting God's forgiveness for me because I chose the *sin in me* to comfort that wound. You might think the first kind of forgiveness would be plenty. It is great to let go of a debt I have been holding against another wounded human being. But I always have found the second kind of forgiveness as necessary as it is harder. Necessary because the enemy would like to steal all the joy out of my life for being unable to do what only God can do in me. Forgiving myself is really only accepting what God has done. Not accepting forgiveness for myself holds on to the sneaking lie that I still owe God something. God tells me I am done with my past way of living and that includes owning a guilt debt already paid for by the cross.

Then do whatever God shows you. What he says may not at this moment seem sensible to you. "This is going to kill me to do it," you think. You may be saying you are not able to do what God wants. You would be right. You cannot. But He can. This is what grace is all about. You need to say to God, "I will respond to what you show me, but you will have to show up with power or I can never do it." His promise of grace means that He will show up as you by faith take up your mat. This is practicing appropriation.

But what God does not promise is that every mat-carrying scenario will lead to a happily-ever-after moment. God has what some people call a helicopter view of things. He can see the past, the present ad the future all at once. Because He has this eternal perspective and knows everything, He may ask you to do some things that result in failure from your point of view. You won't see an reward during your lifetime on earth for your faith act. Underline that. Your friends will not always understand why you changed. You may never master that skill you lack. People will not always apologize. You will not always get better grades. Your parent's divorce will stay final. You may still be plagued with health issues. Like Paul in 2 Corinthians 12, you may still have a thorn in your flesh. Understand that God is not asking you to trust Him to make things turn out the way it seems right to you. He is asking you to trust Him—period.

If you do, what you will get is contentment, because you will come to see that God has everything you need for your restoration in His hands. So whether you are in need or have plenty, hungry or well fed, you will find you can do everything you need to do through His strength (Philippians 4:11-13).

At a deeper level, taking up your mat means you will open the door for God to enter the secret regions of your heart. If He asks to see your darkest secrets, to examine your most painful memories, to heal the unhealable as well as to reign over the addictions that own you, you say 'Yes.' You may not fully understand the implications of the question "Do you want to get well?" But in the end it doesn't matter. You will discover God is safe. And He invites you to pursue intimacy with Him so that you can know this for yourself.

WHAT HEALTH LOOKS LIKE

Maya had been afraid. She is afraid no longer. God has taken away the anxiety caused by her abandonment by her mother and the bullying by her father. They no longer defined her future. It isn't just that she feels lighter and more alive. She is able to trust people around her for the first time in her life. To face her fears without giving in to them. To have deep relationships as a partner rather than a parasite.

Carlos had tried to be perfect so that he would never get into trouble. In the past he had been devastated when he was called out for his behavior by teachers or the boss for small infractions. He would call himself names, and be out of his mind with terror that his parents would punish him when they found out. God has calmed these fears. He now takes his mistakes in stride. Laughs at himself. Respects but does not fear authorities around him. Finds that he can have an adult relationship with his parents.

Like these two, I know you also can get well. You can be freed from your anxiety and fears. Maybe you cannot see this so clearly now. But you can trust God in this. God never changes his mind about you, never deserts you in the middle of your struggle to trust him to heal and deliver you.

One of the most meaningful stories of this truth in the Bible is Jesus' two fishing encounters with Peter. What many people do not realize about Peter was how young he was. You may have seen pictures of him showing him to be an old man, but he was probably barely out of his teens, newly married, when he became a disciple.

In Luke 5, Peter and his crew had been fishing all night without catching so much as an old boot. He then allows Jesus to use his boat as a speaker's platform to address a large crowd that had gathered on the beach to hear Jesus teach. Afterward, Jesus suggests that Peter take his boat out deeper and throw out his nets again. Mildly protesting, Peter does this and is surprised by the catch of a lifetime.

Peter suddenly understands who he is dealing with and he sees his soul naked before Jesus. This is not just another man who has a knack for speaking, a religious teacher who wows people with his insights. Peter perceives that Jesus is someone who possesses such a connection with God that he knows things beyond the ordinary, including the hidden part of Peter. He goes to his knees before Jesus and says, "Go away! Lord, I am a sinful man."

Here is this skilled fisherman suddenly finding he can no longer live with his self-deception. Why? Not because of anything Jesus says, but because of who Jesus is. The contrast between Peter and what he sees in Jesus makes it plain to him that he is not who he is meant to be in spite of his fishing business success. This encounter overwhelms him.

But Jesus is the safest person ever. He is not put off by Peter's dramatic appeal. "I am going to make you a fisher of men," Jesus announces. In other words, Jesus is saying, "I am going to make you whole and let the real person you are be used to change others."

Peter may have known about his brokenness long before his incredible fishing encounter with Jesus. But when Jesus showed up— not in judgment, but with a humorous way to pay for his boat rental—

Peter took his first step towards wholeness on the Galilean Sea. But it would not be his last.

Fast forward to the second Jesus and Peter fishing encounter told in John 21. It was after Jesus' resurrection. Peter had played the worst version of himself and famously denied Jesus three times in spite of his insistence that he would be the only one to stay faithful. On this day Peter had gathered a bunch of his fishing buddies who were hard at work trying to catch fish to sell. You read that right. Peter was not merely on a vacation. He was back to his trade even though by all accounts Jesus had already been seen by him right after rising from the dead. Peter, after his failure, must have reasoned that Jesus had no future use for him. What he had done was failed on a grand scale. Jesus may have forgiven him, but going back into the fishing business was the only option he thought he had left.

I love this story because what happens next is a repeat of the first encounter in Luke 5. The experienced fishermen had caught no fish. The guy on the shore suggests they cast the nets out on the other side. A second catch of a lifetime threatens to break their net. Jesus is finally recognized. Peter immediately swims to shore to be with Jesus. How could he not? Could anything that Jesus did have more meaning to him than this repeat miracle? And what was the point of Jesus following up with questioning three times whether Peter loved him?

Here's my take. "Peter, you thought you knew yourself. You saw yourself as faithful even to the point of dying with me. You were trusting in your own strength to change yourself and Satan knew it. He asked to test your faithfulness. You failed. That was not a surprise because you loved yourself more than you loved me. You know this now. But you are changed now and you will never be the same again.

Our relationship has not ended and I didn't change my plan to make you a fisher of men. Never forget that. Come follow me."

The next thing you know, Peter is boldly speaking in public about Jesus on the Pentecost feast day. Then we find Peter is leading the church in Jerusalem. People are getting healed by him. Transformation happens.

We are all like the fisherman version of Peter. When Jesus first found us, we were a mess. But he has us on a journey of his own design, planning to transform us so that we will be able to fulfill our life's purposes. Jesus, the Father, and the Spirit are all in this process with you and me. God is relentlessly holding on to you because He alone can make you whole—and He wants it for you more than you want it for yourself.

And you will get well! So what will you look like when you get well? What does health look like? Here are three signs of wellness that I have seen in myself.

I no longer feel the pain of past events, no matter how damaging they were at the time. I don't even feel drawn to comfort myself with damaging behavior because of those events. I was talking about a bad event from my childhood one day to my wife, who broke in with, "I am surprised. You don't even sound upset anymore." I told her there was no ache left from that story. God had taken it away long ago. You will find that to be true for you as well.

Healing also gave me compassion for the people who hurt me. Instead of being their victim, I realized how broken their own lives were—how much they had missed out on love and freedom and happiness because of their own unfinished business. It was like cooling lotion on a hot burn inside me. Seeing their brokenness allowed me to forgive them at a depth I never had been able to before. This, too, is real freedom.

Becoming whole myself changes how I see and relate to other people as well. You start understanding that everyone you meet has a lot of unfinished business which is messing them up. As you heal, you want the same for them.

This is different from just being a rescuer. I meet people all the time who want to help hurting people mostly because they themselves are hurting. They attach people to themselves, using these people to bring comfort to the rescuer instead of leading them to real healing. Rescuers are really only inserting themselves into the lives of the rescued to make them feel good about themselves.

As I was healed and delivered, I stopped being a rescuer. I became a better friend, more engaged in pointing others to the path to finding health instead of spending time in self-pity or judging others so I would feel better about myself. I didn't try to rescue people, but I did point them to the same God who rescued me. It still amazes me how God has used me to see others become whole.

This change in me did not all happen overnight. Nor am I saying that I never have a bad day, or even that I no longer have unfinished business. This is a lifelong journey. But I am not broken like I was before. Not anxious. Not fearful. I'm experiencing deep friendships that are healthy instead of destructive—the very things I lacked before I started on this journey with God.

And God will do the same for you.

What is God prompting you to do next?

Like the man beside the pool who picked up his mat and walked, as soon as He tells you what it is…

Just do it.

ꓤESTAꓤT

Small Group Study Guide

Dr. Steve Smith

If you are the leader of the small group study, you can download the complimentary *Restart Small Group Leaders Guide* at www.ChurchEquippers.com/downloadables/

WELCOME TO THE SMALL GROUP EXPERIENCE

THIS EXPERIENCE CONTAINS 10 weekly sessions. To be a participant, you must already be a Christian and part of a church family. Without the presence of the Spirit in your life, you will not be able to understand the deep truths of the Sessions.

For this experience to be most effective for you, you should be part of a group of 8 or less that only has guys or girls in it. Many of the Sessions ask for personal information that would be difficult to share in front of those of the opposite sex.

The following Sessions are full of the questions that you will need to answer. They will help you to be prepared to address the unfinished business you have that God reveals to you during this study. Make sure to write out answers to the questions so you will be ready to share your thoughts with the others in your group. Bring a Bible so you can look up the Scriptures during your time together. Then you can see for yourself that what God has said has authority and meaning for your life.

It is important for you do the homework. You will not grow through these sessions if you don't do it. Each homework assignment is to prepare you for the next session. Not being prepared says you may not be ready to be healed and set free yet.

I hope you will hear God speaking to you during this experience. He loves you unconditionally and has already determined He is going to make you like Jesus. Listen to Him carefully.

Peace! Dr. Steve

Session 1: The Power To Change Is Yours

1. The Heart Chart is about everyone's journey in life. It shows the inner turmoil people experience by living in a broken world. Every person you meet is wounded and every person has chosen sin to comfort themselves. But wherever you are on the Heart Chart, God is with you.

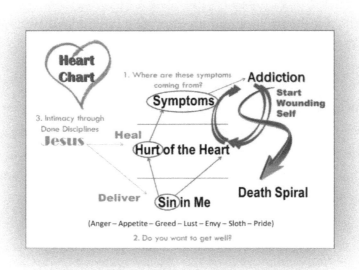

- What do you see has been produced from being wounded and choosing sin in me to comfort your pain?
- How has it affected your life?

2. John 10:10 tells us that "The thief comes only to steal and kill and destroy; I have come that they may have life, and have it to the full."

- Who is the thief who is stealing and destroying your life?
- Do you know what he uses to destroy you?
- What is he taking from you?
- What would it mean for you to have the full life that Jesus came to give you instead?
- Go back to the Heart Chart and look at what Jesus does when he gives you this life. How would his healing and delivering change your life?

3. In Romans 8:29, Paul explains how God is actively at work changing us. He says, "God knew what he was doing from the very beginning. He decided from the outset to shape the lives of those who love him along the same lines as the life of his Son. The Son stands first in the line of humanity he restored. We see the original and intended shape of our lives there in him." (Message)
- What makes Jesus different?
- There is a difference between trying to reform your life to live like Jesus and being transformed by God to be like Jesus.

   REFORM = God's truth lived out by my strength

   TRANSFORM = God's truth lived out by the empowering presence of the Spirit.

4. How would you be different when God changes you to be like Jesus?

5. Do you have a hard time believing God wants to change you? If so, why? If not, what will be your next step in allowing Jesus to heal and free you?

SESSION 1 HOMEWORK ASSIGNMENT

In the next session, you will be studying the way you got into your mess. To prepare for this Session, please make a private list of everyone you have a broken or strained relationship with, including God. Ask God why each relationship was strained or broken.

SESSION 2: WHY WE STRUGGLE IN OUR MESS

1. What does your list of broken or strained relationships tell you about where you are?

2. Read the Garden story of Genesis 3:1-19. In what ways are your strained/broken relationships related to the Garden story?

   - What happened to you because of Adam and Eve's choice to eat of the tree?

   - How does possessing the knowledge of good and evil create problems between you and the other people in your life?

   - How have these strained/broken relationships affected how you feel about yourself?

   - Are there areas in your life where doing what you prefer, such as defiance, unforgiveness, going your own way, etc., brought more damage to your strained/broken relationships?

   - Do you believe that these strained/broken relationships will go on for the rest of your life? If no, what will need to heal in you to change the strained/broken relationships that you currently have?

3. In Hebrews 10:14-17, the writer tells us, "For by one sacrifice (of Jesus on the cross) God has made whole forever those who are being made holy. The Holy Spirit also testifies to us about this. First he says: "This is the covenant I will make with them after that time, says the Lord. I will put my laws in their hearts, and I will write them on their minds." Then he adds: "Their sins and lawless acts I will remember no more."

   This means that, through the sacrifice of Jesus on the cross, God made a covenant with broken people like us. Covenant making is about creating an unbreakable relationship between those who are part of it.

- According to the writer, what has God already done by making covenant with you?
- How does this help you understand His love for you?
- If you have been made whole already by God, how will being made holy affect you?
- How do you see this affecting how you live your life and your relationships?

4. Romans 12:2 says "Do not conform to the pattern of this world, but be transformed by the renewing of your mind." Paul talks about transformation as taking place in the mind.

The lies that you may believe about yourself and others reveal that Satan has gotten to you through your mind. You may be repeating these lies to yourself on a daily basis. Renewing of your mind involves the lies of the enemy being rooted out by the truth of who God is and your relationship to Him. You cooperate with the Holy Spirit in this process by:

- Recognizing and naming the lie.
- Replacing it with God's truth, even when your emotions are rejecting this. Truth comes when the Spirit makes the revelation about God clear to you.
- Living the truth by the power of the Holy Spirit.
  Process how this could change how you see yourself and the people with whom you are in a strained or broken relationship.

SESSION 2 HOMEWORK ASSIGNMENT

The next session is about your true identity as sons and daughters of God. To prepare, please read through Colossians 1-3, looking for (and maybe highlighting) every place it says you are "in Christ, or in Jesus, or in him" or "with Christ, or with Jesus, or with him." These two phrases are Paul's shorthand way of talking about your true identity. As you spot each one, write out the truth you discover by using the following statement:

In Christ I am (or I have)_____.

Examples:

1:5   I have hope stored up for me in Heaven in Christ Jesus.

1:11   I am strengthened with all power according to His glorious might in Christ Jesus.

Session 3: Identity In Christ

WHO AM I?

1. The story of the Garden in Genesis 2-3 shows that we are the descendants of Adam. The story of the gospel tells us we are now children of God. Paul uses the phrase "in Christ" many times in his writing to express this truth. So who are you "in Christ" and what do you have?

2. This Circle of Transformation illustrates what your journey is all about.

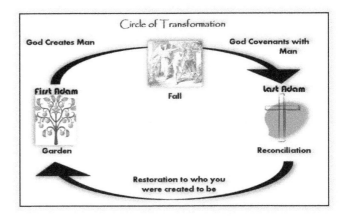

- Before the first Adam messed up, what was his relationship with God like, according to Genesis 2:7-25?

- What does being messed up by Adam and Eve's choices mean in light of Genesis 3:8-10, "Then the man and his wife heard the sound of the Lord God as he was walking in the garden in the cool of the day, and they hid from the Lord God among the trees of the garden. But the Lord God called to the man,

'Where are you?' Adam answered, 'I heard you in the garden, and I was afraid because I was naked; so I hid.'"

- How does Adam's choice affect you personally?
- What does God offer you through the Last Adam?
- How does the Last Adam's choice affect you personally?

3. Proverbs 27:19 says, "As a face is reflected in water, so the heart reflects the person." There is stuff going on inside of your heart, some of which you won't even admit to yourself—let alone anyone else.

- Why might you be afraid to reveal what you struggle with inside?
- How might this kind of secrecy affect your journey to wholeness?
- How has being in Jesus changed this for you and others who believe?

4. Romans 6:1-6 (pictured below) explains how you being "in Christ" has changed you more deeply than you may have thought.

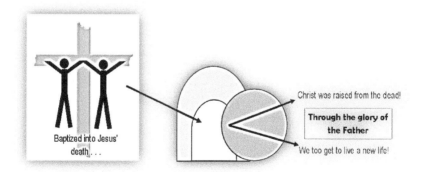

- What do these verses say about how this change in who you are was accomplished?
- What does getting to live a new life mean in your personal situation?

SESSION 3 HOMEWORK ASSIGNMENT

In the next session you will examine your symptoms—outward and observable behaviors and attitudes that are causing you pain and/or are barriers between you and others. Using the Symptom Discovery Inventory For Teens and Young Adults, develop a comprehensive a list of your personal symptoms as you are able.

The *Symptom Discovery Inventory For Teens and Young Adults* is available at: <u>www.ChurchEquippers.com/downloadables</u>

SESSION 4: IDENTIFYING YOUR STUFF

1. Read John 10:10-11 again. Jesus came so you would have life to the fullest. What are some of the symptoms—ways you act or think—that keep you from living life to the fullest?
   - Of these personal symptoms, which ones would you say have passed into being addictions—controlling you rather than you controlling them?
   - What parts of your life are being affected by your addictions?
2. Symptoms always indicate deeper issues inside us. Talk about where you think these symptoms/addictions are coming from.
   - How does talking about this subject affect you emotionally?
3. In Romans 8:28-29 (MSG), Paul tells us that the Spirit "knows us far better than we know ourselves, knows our condition, and keeps us present before God. That's why we can be so sure that every detail in our lives of love for God is worked into something good. God knew what he was doing from the very beginning. He decided from the outset to shape the lives of those who love him along the same lines as the life of his Son."
   - Compare your personal identity with that of the character of Jesus. In what way is God at work using your symptoms and addictions to shape you along the same lines as the life of Jesus?
   - What do you need from God to really believe this?
4. Read the story about Jesus healing the man by the pool of Bethesda in John 5:1-16.
   - What was the key question that Jesus asked?
   - Why was that question important?

- What do you think would have happened if the man had said "No"?
- What did the man's response in verse 7 reveal about the man's attempts to get well?
- Why do you think Jesus made him take up his mat on a Sabbath day?
- How do you understand the question Jesus is asking in terms of your own need to get well?
- Where are you personally at in responding to Jesus' question? Which of the following words capture where you are at this moment? Hope. Trust. Fear. Questions. Determination. Anger. Surrender.

6. What would it take for you to be ready to ask God to do a ruthless search of your heart to show you what you need to know to get well?

SESSION 4 HOMEWORK ASSIGNMENT

In the next session you will focus on how and why you are wounded. **Schedule at least an hour to do the Hurt of the Heart Inventory.** *The Hurt of the Heart Inventory for Teens and Young Adults* **is a free download and can be found at:** **www.ChurchEquippers.com/downloadables**

SESSION 5: HURT OF THE HEART

1. When you did the Hurt of the Heart Inventory, did you find it hard to face what you discovered about your emotional history?

   - Do you think that the hurts of your heart that you remember were inflicted deliberately, accidentally, or thoughtlessly?
   - Why do you think the person(s) who inflicted the wounds did that to you?
   - Were you made to "feel" that the wounding was your fault?
   - How has that person(s) actions affected your ability to receive love from him or her?

2. In the Bible the heart is a place where emotions and rational thoughts are weighed out to make decisions about life.

   - What are the implications of the following picture in light of your own life?

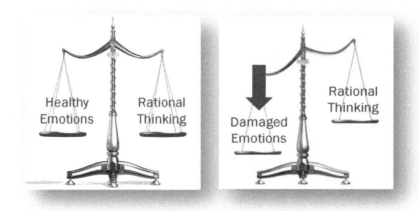

   - Can you think of a decision you made that you now know was directed by your damaged emotions overriding your rational thinking?

- These kinds of decisions are called irrational. Why do you think people still do them if they are irrational?

3. People most often try to deal with wounds internally. In the process, they develop self-talk (Examples: You did it again...Give it up...You are so stupid...I am better than that idiot...I have to use...I have to look...I have to eat...I feel so alone...No one cares about me).

   - What are the words of your self-talk and what does it reveal about how you think about yourself?

   - Which of the following have appeared in your life because of being wounded?

     1) Denial that what happened affected you.

     2) A sense of loss and being a victim.

     3) A belief that you are powerless to do anything to get over it.

     4) A determination to prove yourself.

4. Were you a Christian at the time when you received the wounds you remember? If you were, how did the wounds affect your relationship with God?

5. What do you understand has to happen between you and God in order for you to move towards healing?

SESSION 5 HOMEWORK ASSIGNMENT

In the next session you will work through sin choices that damage us. Please schedule time to do the Deadly Sin Inventory. It will take maybe 30-60 minutes, so make sure to allow enough time to do it. *The Deadly Sin Inventory for Teens and Young Adults* is available as a free download at:

www.ChurchEquippers.com/downloadables

SESSION 6: SIN IN ME

1. What is the difference between comforting yourself and being healed of the pain you feel inside?

   - After doing the Deadly Sin Inventory, what deadly sin(s) did you discover you were comforting yourself with?

   - How did your pre-inventory lineup compare with your actual results?

   - Was it hard for you to accept the results of this inventory? If so, why?

2. In Romans 7:14-23, What does Paul reveal about his own journey towards being shaped along the same lines as Jesus?

   - What is the difference between sins that we do and the sin that is inside you?

   - Why do you think people prefer to choose sin over being made whole?

3. On the following chart are the two things you need Jesus to do for you. Which is the harder one for you to believe he can do?

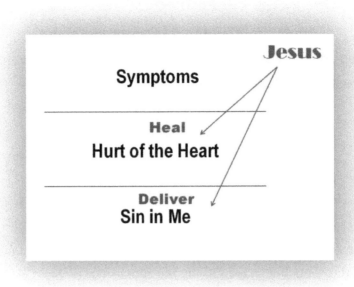

- Count the cost on this question. What do you really want to do about your inside issues? Do you really want to get well?

4. James 5:16 says "Therefore confess your sins to each other and pray for each other so that you may be healed."

- Why do you think confession leads to healing?
- What are the *sin in me* choices which you are aware you have made that you need Jesus to deliver you from? Are you ready to confess and repent of these choices?
- Do you understand what "repentance" means?

5. Paul teaches in Galatians 5:22-25 that God is making us different from what we were when deadly sin controlled us, "But the fruit of the Spirit is love, joy, peace, forbearance, kindness, goodness, faithfulness, gentleness and self-control. Against such things there is no law. Those who belong to Christ Jesus have crucified the

flesh with its passions and desires. Since we live by the Spirit, let us keep in step with the Spirit."

- How is the fruit of the Spirit different from the deadly sin that has been controlling your life?
- How will keeping in step with the Spirit bring change and wholeness to your life?

6. This fruit is called The Great Exchange. Look up 2 Corinthians 5:21.

- What is being exchanged in this verse?
- Which word would connect to the fruit of the Spirit?

SESSION 6 HOMEWORK ASSIGNMENT

This is a different kind of assignment. This week, when you spend time alone with God, you are to take a full 60 seconds and be quiet before the Father. This is not a prayer time, but a listening/receiving time from God. Start by reading Hebrews 4:14-16. As you are ready, recognize you are in God's presence. Tell Him you are ready to receive from Him whatever He has for you. Be quiet and listen for His voice. After the time is finished, write out what you experienced in that time. Practice being in His presence in this way every day this week.

Session 7: Intimacy Through Rest

1. Paul prays in Ephesians 1:17 an *intimacy prayer*—that God would "give you the Spirit of wisdom and revelation so that you may know Him better." How do people generally come to know someone else better?

2. What do Jesus' words in Matthew 11:28-30 reveal about why he wants you to come and be with him?

3. The writer of Hebrews states "Let us then approach God's throne of grace with confidence, so that we may receive mercy and find grace to help us in our time of need." (Hebrews 4:16).

   - Did you feel safe to be with God when you spent time in quiet before Him this week?

   - What did you learn about being with God just to receive something from Him?

4. Spend the next ten minutes resting in God's presence. Three things to keep in mind as God gives rest for your soul:

   - **First:** *Approach* God within yourself without fear of rejection. This takes humility. Your right to go into God's presence is not based on whether you were good or bad. You have no right on your own. But by His own choice He is inviting you. He wants you. And He has paid the price to remove all the barriers between you and Him. It's a humbling thing to go before God and say, "Here I am. I'm your child."

   - **Second:** *Believe* that He is with you and you are with Him. And that He is delivering what you need. You need mercy, compassion, comfort and affection. And you need grace—the power to do what God has for you to do.

- **Third:** *Receive* tenderness (mercy) and power (grace) even when you feel you deserve His judgment.

5. One important impact of the process is changing your belief about how you see God as the Father. This is about seeing Him as He is, rather than the image you have projected on Him out of your fears and rebellion. One of the sources for your false image of God is your parents. How might your view of your father, mother or whoever raised you, or even a pastor or teacher cloud your understanding of God?
   - Read Elijah's story in 1 Kings 19:1-18.
     - What happened to Elijah before he actually was ready to hear from God?
     - What do you think the wind, the earthquake and the fire in the story tell you about how we view God?

CONCLUDING STATEMENTS TO BE READ ALOUD

1) Understand this—you will not grow in your ability to rest by a quick session or two with God.

2) Being with God without an agenda so you can hear and receive from Him has a learning curve.

3) You have to set aside time intentionally and you must get away from distractions.

4) It may take months before you begin to sense you truly are ready to hear God when you are with Him. Why? Because we have busy minds. Instead of the ability to listen in quiet, we have cultivated a brain geared to short bursts of focus and multitasking.

5) Do not give up this means of pursuing God. He is already there, and ready for you to know Him better.

6) He has also given you His Spirit so this can be real in your life.

7) Practice. Listen. Wait. Rest.

8) In time, as you do this *consistently*, you will begin to have the kind of relationship with God you have always wanted, and more.

SESSION 7 HOMEWORK ASSIGNMENT

In the next session you will learn a second practice that God offers you to bring transformation into your life—Appropriation (which means grabbing hold of what God has stored in your spiritual 'refrigerator'). In preparation for this session, read the following verses (Romans 5:10; Romans 6:4; Galatians 2:20; Colossians 3:1-4) and think on this question: How can I experience the reality of Christ living out his life in me? Continue practicing your 60 second daily listening and receiving times with God. This will help to establish a lifetime habit.

SESSION 8: INTIMACY THROUGH APPROPRIATION

1. What have you learned from God so far? How has this new knowledge affected you emotionally? Spiritually?

2. Study the following chart.

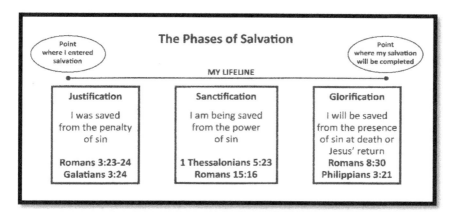

- Where are you in the salvation process right now?
- What does that tell you about what God is doing in you?

3. The second prayer Paul prays in Ephesians 1:18-19 is an *insight prayer*. He is praying that his readers would know through experience three things that they have been given by God as a result of putting their faith in Jesus. What are the hope, riches and power you have been given according to this passage?

   - Compare these verses with Ephesians 1:3 and 2 Peter 1:3-4. In what way has God equipped you to be saved from the power of sin? What do you get to do instead of having to sin?

   - When you are being tempted or are under spiritual attack, do you need to ask God to give you something more than He has already given you?

- What do you understand 'appropriate' to mean for yourself?
- Have you ever been denied something that was yours?
- How does having hope, riches and power make a difference for your faith journey?

4. Look up John 1:33, 14:25-26; Ephesians 1:13; Acts 1:8; 2:38; Romans 8:9-11; 2 Corinthians 3:17-19 and answer the following question: How is receiving the Spirit the gamechanger in Jesus living his life out in us?
   - How does having the Spirit explain the difference between being reformed in your character and being transformed to be like Jesus?

5. You are not just becoming a better person, but the Spirit is developing Jesus' attributes in you as your personal character. How does transformation differ from any self-improvement course you might try?

6. Dig a little deeper. What issue are you aware of in your faith journey right now for which you need to exercise appropriation?

SESSION 8 HOMEWORK ASSIGNMENT

Continue practicing your 60 second daily listening and receiving times with God.

In the next session, you will learn a third practice that God offers you to bring transformation into your life—*meditation on the love of God*. Take time this week to get apart from all of life's distractions. In the quiet, focus your mind on how much God loves you.

Session 9: Intimacy Through Meditation On God's Love

1. What have you learned from God so far? How has this new knowledge affected you emotionally? Spiritually?

2. Do this Envelope Exercise: Get four envelopes and 1 slip of paper.

   - Write "Jesus" on the piece of paper. Write your name on one envelope, "Jesus Christ" on the second envelope, "The Father" on the third envelope and "The Holy Spirit" on the last envelope.

   - Look up 1 John 4:4, 15. Place the piece of paper marked "Jesus" into the envelope with your name on it. Write under your name on the envelope "God in the person of Jesus lives in me."

   - Look up Ephesians 2:6 and Colossians 2:6. Fold and place the first envelope inside the second envelope marked "Jesus Christ." Write "I am in Jesus."

   - Look up John 17:20-23. Fold and place the second envelope inside the third envelope marked with "The Father." Write "Jesus is in the Father."

   - Look up Ephesians 1:13. Fold and place the third envelope inside the fourth envelope marked "The Holy Spirit." Write on flap "I am sealed in the Holy Spirit."
     1) Where are you?
     2) Where is God?
     3) How safe are you?
     4) How does this illustration of Bible truth allow you to appropriate hope when Satan throws lies at you?

3. In Paul's transformational prayer in Ephesians 3, he prays, "I pray that you, being rooted and established in love, may have power, together with all the Lord's holy people, to grasp how wide and long and high and deep is the love of Christ, and to know this love that surpasses knowledge—that you may be filled to the measure of all the fullness of God."

   - Why does Paul want people to know this love of Christ that they are already rooted and established in?
   - The way you deepen your grasp on God's love is through meditating on the love of Christ. Meditation is possible when you step away from all of life's distractions. In the quiet, you *focus* your mind, not *empty* your mind. This is the critical difference between Christian mediation and eastern mystic meditation.
   - Spend the next ten minutes resting in God's presence. During this time, ask God to give you a grasp on *one* of the following:
     1) How much God loves you.
     2) Why God chooses to love you.
     3) How much God loves even those who wounded you.

4. What did you learn during this time of meditation?

   - How do you think that this deepening intimacy with God will help you in the face of the accusations, temptations and lies of the enemy?
   - How do you think that this deepening intimacy with God will help you really forgive the people who wounded you?

5. Read Matthew 6:12, 14; Mark 11:24-26. Forgiveness is at the heart of unbroken intimacy with God. For what person(s) do you need to trust God to give you true forgiveness so you can continue to deepen your intimacy with Him?

- What do you need from God so that you will be able to forgive the person(s) who wounded you?
- What help do you need from others to move forward in forgiveness?

SESSION 9 HOMEWORK ASSIGNMENT

- Continue practicing your 60 second daily listening and receiving times with God.
- In the next session you are preparing yourself for going on in your faith journey applying the truths you have learned through this study. To be ready for this last Session, read through Matthew 5:3-10, which are the eight Beatitudes that Jesus taught at the beginning of what we call the Sermon on the Mount. Be ready to discuss the Beatitude that is most challenging for you.

SESSION 10: CONTINUING WITH YOUR FAITH JOURNEY

1. Which Beatitude is most challenging to understand for you?
2. The order of the Beatitudes in Matthew 5:3-10 suggests a progressive transformation process, starting with acknowledging that you have nothing in you that will make you into the person God created you to be. This is not just a one-time occurrence, but is a recurring cycle in your transformational process. You will need to continually come back again to this point—refusing to believe the lie that the *hurt of the heart* which is at the center of your mind at this moment can be dealt with by anything other than God Himself. You are then ready to humbly allow Him to free you from the power of *sin in me* choices by focusing on intimacy with Him. Never forget that it is God who is going to develop these in you— you can't possibly do it yourself. Walk through the eight Beatitudes together and discuss what they mean for your faith journey.
    a) **Poor In Spirit:** *Being Humbled by My Spiritual Poverty*, which is the point at which you recognize you have neither the ability within yourself—nor the power—to remake yourself into the person you were created to be.
    b) **Mourn:** *Grieving Properly* over the wounds you have received from living in a fallen world, while recognizing that you have, in turn, wounded others as well.
    c) **Meek:** *Submitting Totally* to the reign of God over you so that you can live in this world the way you were intended to live by God.
    d) **Hunger and Thirst:** *Refocusing Desires* toward wanting what God wants, allowing yourself to be restored to the likeness of His Son.

e) **Merciful:** *Growing Compassion* for those who are wounded, including those who wounded you.

f) **Pure In Heart:** *Seeing God Clearly* to the point that you stop projecting false images on Him drawn from your experiences with human figures of authority, including your parents, and stop believing lies about Him due to these false images.

g) **Peacemakers:** *Conforming to Jesus* who is your peace, and who is the one who offers peace and restoration to all who have rebelled and rejected God.

h) **Persecuted:** *Anticipating Opposition* from friends, family and even religious people as you progressively are becoming the person you were created to be.

- Why do you think you need to recognize that your faith journey will be a progressive one?
- Look up Revelation 12:10. If you experience failure along this faith journey, who will be the one who will accuse you and seek to use your failure against you?
- According to Romans 8:31-34, what will be God's attitude and action towards you?
- Do you think there will come a time when Satan's lies can no longer draw you back into destructive behavior and distrust of God? Why or why not?
- Why, then, should you personally have mercy on others around you, even those who you consider bad people?
- What would mercy look like?

3. Look up 1 Corinthians 2:10-16 and answer the following question: Why has God given us His Spirit?

- How does this truth connect to keeping in step with the Spirit (Galatians 5:25)?
- How far have you come in learning to trust the Spirit's work in you?
- Reflect back to the story about the man who had been sick for 38 years Jesus encountered beside the pool of Bethesda. Picking up the mat was Jesus' invitation to get well. Picking up your mat is doing what God is telling you to do at this moment. What mat is God telling you to pick up?

4. How do you plan to go on from here? Discuss the following practical steps:
- How will I seek to make what I learned during these sessions part of my own life?
- How do I plan to incorporate the "Done" Disciplines regularly into my faith journey so that I can grow in my intimacy with God? Who will I ask to help hold me accountable in the initial stages of making these a regular part of my life?
- What aspects of Jesus' life and character should I study to gain insight into what I am to become?
- According to 2 Peter 1:5-9, what else should I seek to see developed in my life so that I can be productive in my faith? How would I go about developing them?
- Who is someone who needs to hear this—with whom I can regularly share what I am learning? When will I start the process?

5. A last point. Look up 1 Peter 5:5b-11.
- What is it that you need most of all in order to access God's grace?

- Why do you need to be self-controlled and pay attention to the activity of the enemy?
- Who is on your side in all this?

ONGOING ASSIGNMENT

- Continue to practice the "Done" Disciplines in pursuit of intimacy with God and the freedom Jesus promised through the gospel ("It is for freedom that Christ has set us free." Galatians 5:1).
- Confess your sins to others in community and be healed.
- Continue practicing your 60 second daily listening and receiving times with God.
- Make these practices a lifelong pursuit!

For additional tools, please visit:

www.ChurchEquippers.com